In the Wake of
Three Men in a Boat

In the same series:

Royal Tunbridge Wells – the History of a Spa Town, by Alan Savidge and Charlie Bell
Royal Visitors to Tunbridge Wells, by Don Foreman

By the same author:
Victorians on the Thames

In the Wake of
Three Men in a Boat

by

R.R. BOLLAND

OAST BOOKS
Tunbridge Wells

First published in the UK by
OAST BOOKS
12 Dene Way
Speldhurst
Tunbridge Wells
Kent TN3 0NX

© R.R. Bolland 1995
ISBN: 1-898594-09-0

A catalogue record for this book is available from the British Library

Printed in Great Britain by
Biddles Ltd, Guildford and King's Lynn

Contents

List of Illustrations

All photographs by the author or from his personal collection. Acknowledgements to Home Publishing Company for Map, p.10.

The chief beauty of this book lies not so much in its literary style, or in the extent and usefulness of the information it conveys, as in its simple truthfulness. Its pages form a record of events that really happened. All that has been done is to colour them, and for this no extra charge has been made. George and Harris and Montmorency are not poetical ideals, but things of flesh and blood – especially George, who weighs about twelve stone. Other works may excel this in depth of thought and knowledge of human nature: other books may rival it in originality and size; but, for hopeless and incurable veracity, nothing yet discovered can surpass it.

Jerome K. Jerome – Preface to the First Edition of
Three Men in a Boat, 1889

REFERENCE

Catchment area of the River Thames ———
  "   "   " " Tributaries ....
Divisional Areas ——————
County Boundaries ————

Scale 0   5   10   15   20 Miles

Based upon the Ordnance Survey map with the permission of the Controller of Her Majesty's Stationery Office. Crown Copyright Reserved.

Introduction

I suppose many visitors to Hampton Court have looked at the red brick wall alongside the Thames, and recalled Jerome K. Jerome's words 'What a dear old wall that is that runs along by the river there! I never pass it without feeling better for the sight of it.'

I, in my turn, never pass it without these words running through my mind. On one such occasion, it occurred to me that his description is as true today as it was when it was written over a century ago. Following this line of thought, I considered the other descriptions of places and things in *Three Men in a Boat*. My job took me up and down the Thames, and on my river journeys I looked for these other places, and tried to visualise any changes since Jerome's day.

Many people who have read and who love *Three Men in a Boat* have discussed the book with me, and it is surprising that most of them believe it to be a work of fiction; not only do they imagine that the incidents related did not actually happen; they doubt whether all the places described are real. I must confess that once I myself regarded some of the events as fictional, made up by Jerome to fit in with the story.

It was at Hampton Court that I decided to investigate the people, places and events described in the book. If the description of the wall was true, how much truth was there in the rest? Being so familiar with the river myself, I knew without searching that the Bull at Sonning and the Barley Mow at Clifton Hampden were not figments of imagination. But what about Mrs Thomas's tomb in Hampton Church, or the dogs' cemetery at Oatlands Park? Even if they had been there in Jerome's day, did they still exist now?

I started to enquire into these two things, and found that almost everything that Jerome had said about them was true. I became more interested and ambitious, and turned my attention to the song 'He's Got 'em On', sung by the 'Arrys and 'Arriets near Cleeve. This, I found, was a real song, published in 1880. My most difficult piece of research was necessary when I decided to find out whether the story of the drowned woman in the river at Basildon was true. After a long search I found out not only her name, but where she is buried, together with her true story, on which Jerome based the brief details he related. And sad as his version is, the full story is very much more pathetic.

This, then, is how I came to write this book. If it were never to have seen the light of day, it would have been worth it. I had the satisfaction of following small clues and proving that certain incidents were true and that certain people actually existed. Whenever I finish reading *Three Men in a Boat* (and I have read it many times), I have a feeling of regret that Jerome did not see fit to make it twice as long. I know that I am being foolish and that it would not be the joy it is if it were changed in any way. Nevertheless, it has given me pleasure to discover more about some of the places that Jerome loved, and to visit them today and see how little they have changed. And I hope I am not alone in thinking that it is of interest to know that some of the people mentioned, who up to now have been considered fictional, did in fact exist, and that their otherwise unimportant lives were, for a brief moment, spotlighted in *Three Men in a Boat*.

It is possible that many who love the book have no wish to enquire further; but I hope that there may be some who are as inquisitive as I about these matters, for I would feel less selfish if a few others could share my pleasure.

PART ONE
THE JOURNEY

The Journey

NB By convention, the left and right banks of the Thames are defined from the viewpoint of the downstream traveller.

The station at Kingston-Upon-Thames, where Jerome, Harris and Montmorency arrived on the train that was supposed to be the Exeter Mail, is half a mile from the river. Flys met the trains and we can assume the travellers, loaded as they were with bags, hampers and rugs, hired one to take them to the water. Jerome tells us it was a glorious morning, and as the horse trotted along the quiet, dusty road they no doubt looked forward eagerly to getting on to the river. Nowadays they would have a longer journey, and a less peaceful one, for one-way traffic has come to Kingston, and along the former country lane cars roar and rush three and four abreast. Chapters 5-6

Jerome referred to the 'magnificent carved oak staircase in one of the houses of Kingston. It is a shop now, in the market place, but it was evidently once the mansion of some great personage.' And then he told the story of his friend who, as a reward for paying promptly for a hat, was taken by the shopmen to see the staircase and a room with carved oak panelling that had been covered with wallpaper. Chapter 6

The shop referred to was Hide & Co., which occupied the site from about 1740 until the 1970s. When I visited the shop some twenty-five years ago, it had developed from the tailors and drapers business of Jerome's time into a modern department store and the staircase was in full and unfettered use, giving public access to the electrical department. It is indeed a magnificent staircase, with a wealth of fine Jacobean carving including grotesque human figures, the infant Bacchus, bunches of grapes and other scenes evoking the days when it formed the central feature of the Castle Inn (*Plate 1*). Kingston Heritage have informed me that the premises are now temporarily empty, and may be redeveloped; it is to be hoped that, whatever changes take place, the staircase will occupy an honoured and unique place in any new development.

There being no information about the room with oak panelling that Jerome alleged had been covered with wallpaper, it seemed that he had used his imagination and embellished the story of the existing staircase with the non-existent panelling. But the book's 'simple

15

truthfulness' was confirmed by the following paragraph taken from a late Victorian book *Greater London*.

> In the market place there is a shop, kept by Mr Chilcott, a tailor and draper, which looks as if it had been built since Her Majesty's [Queen Victoria's] accession. Its walls and beams, however, are certainly as old as the reign of Elizabeth, though the panelling of the former is concealed by paper.

Here is proof that there was a panelled room in those days in addition to the staircase and that, as in the story, the carved wood had been covered with wallpaper. Hide & Co. were unable to say what happened to the panelling; in fact they stated that there had never been any story handed down about oak panelling, and they surmised that it might have been sold by some person more concerned with making money than conserving beauty. The staircase itself was moved several times within the building and it appears likely that it was during one of these periods of rebuilding that the panelling was removed.

According to an article in the *Surrey Comet*, which was published in 1898, 'Jerome K. Jerome, too, in his "Three Men in a Boat" also makes mention of this remarkable staircase with his characteristic humour, and this alone, if nothing else, would serve to give it world-wide notice.' *Three Men* was published in book form only nine years before this was written, and it is a remarkable tribute to the popularity of the book. Even in that short time it had become a classic.

Jerome, Harris and Montmorency stepped into their boat in front of ancient boathouses and the one they almost certainly left from, Turks, still exists. This area forms an enclave charged with Victorian atmosphere in stark contrast to the ultra modern development close by (*Plate 11*).

Much of the present-day scenery between Kingston Bridge and Hampton Court would be familiar to Jerome. Surbiton Promenade on the left is still there (it used to be known as Surbiton Parade). There are some large houses built early in this century, on land which formed part of the Ditton Hall estate, and these would be new to him, as would the numerous bungalows on the island at Thames Ditton.

On the Middlesex shore there has been practically no change, with the towpath beside the river, and the wide stretch of land reaching back to the fence and wall of Home Park, part of the Hampton Court Estate. A winding track wends its way between mature trees and not even the sound of boat engines on the nearby river can dispel the Victorian atmosphere. In places the stream itself is screened by shrubs and trees along its edge. It will be remembered that after they rammed the bank owing to Jerome's inattention, he got out and towed the boat past Hampton Court. The river bank here, in common with the rest of the towpath bank, would have been kept completely clear of

Chapter 6

1. The staircase at Hide & Co., Kingston upon Thames (by permission of Kingston Heritage)

2. The maze, Hampton Court

3. The dogs' cemetery, Oatlands Park

4. Thames swans

5. Boulter's Lock

6. Below Boulter's Lock, 1880s

7. The Grotto, Basildon

8. Greenlands, above Hambleden Lock

obstructions, and were Jerome to see the towpath today he would no doubt comment upon the numerous trees and shrubs along its edge.

The wall, so vividly described, still divides the towpath from the gardens at Hampton Court. 'Such a mellow, bright, sweet old wall; what a charming picture it would make, with the lichen creeping here and the moss growing there, a shy young vine peeping over the top at this spot, to see what is going on upon the busy river, and the sober old ivy clustering a little further down! There are fifty shades and tints and hues in every ten yards of that old wall.' The next time you have the chance to walk along that part of the towpath, look at that wall and see how little it has changed over the years (*Plates 9 and 10*). Parts of the brick-work could date from the same period as the earliest part of the Palace, i.e. 1514, but as it has been regularly maintained, it is not possible to put an exact date on any part of it. But a hundred years are a comparatively short period in the life of such an ancient monument, and we can be sure that the wall we see today is very much the same as when it was seen and described by Jerome.

Jerome and Harris did not visit the maze on the journey described in *Three Men in a Boat*. It was on a previous occasion that Harris, accompanied by his cousin, entered the maze with the intention of walking round for ten minutes and then getting some lunch; Jerome describes the amusing events that followed. The entrance fee of 2d which would have been paid by Harris has now, incidentally, increased to £1.75 (*Plate 2*).

Jerome towed past Hampton Court. At the bridge, which in those days, according to Dickens Junior's *Dictionary of the Thames*, was 'an ugly iron erection', he would have got into the skiff and pulled across the river to Molesey Lock, for the towpath changes sides here. The present bridge, of red brick, was opened in 1932, and is a great improvement on its predecessor.

Jerome commented on the size of Molesey Lock (spelt Moulsey at that time) and surmised that it was the busiest lock on the river. In those days the lock was the original structure, built of wood and opened in 1815. The present lock replaced the old one in 1906. The boat rollers were there in Jerome's day, and they were used very much more than they are today.

Chapter 7

This is not surprising, for we see in old photographs that Jerome was not exaggerating when he tells us that on occasions the river from Hampton Court Palace to Hampton Church was a mass of boats waiting to pass up or down through the lock. Granted that Molesey Lock was large, in those conditions there would have been a strong inducement to use the rollers and bypass the crowded lock.

The towpath runs on the right from Hampton Court Bridge to Walton Bridge, skirting Molesey and Sunbury locks. To avoid any confusion, right and left are defined from the point of view of the downstream traveller and I have abided by this convention, despite the upstream progress of the Three Men for much of the book.

Hampton Church stands facing the river; with its tower crowned by four pinnacles, it is familiar to all river men (*Plate 12*). The church is so prominent that Jerome had little chance of passing it without Harris, who had a weakness for such things, wanting to get out and see the graves. One feels that even the expedient adopted so successfully at Shepperton of knocking Harris' cap into the water would not have worked at Hampton. The church seems to have more than its fair share of monuments, and the best known of these thanks to Jerome is 'Mrs Thomas's tomb'. Throughout the length of the Thames, a mention in *Three Men in a Boat* of a church or an inn is usually regarded as a cachet for it, and it is rare for those interested in the subject so honoured to omit to mention it. The guide to Hampton Parish Church (St Mary's) tells us that the monument referred to is along the south aisle, against the east wall. Under a photograph of the tomb is the following quotation:

Chapter 7   'Harris wanted to get out at Hampton Church, to go and see Mrs Thomas's tomb. "Who is Mrs Thomas?" I asked. "How should I know?" replied Harris. "She's a lady that's got a funny tomb, and I want to see it." '

Susanna Thomas, who died in 1731, was the only daughter of Sir Dalby Thomas, Governor of the African Company's settlements. The sculpture was by Sir Henry William Powell, and it represents Susanna reading to her mother. I have been unable to find out why it is known as Mrs Thomas's tomb, when it relates to a Miss Thomas.

If you visit the church to look for this monument take care not to be misled by the one in the south porch, which is an effigy of Dame Sibil Penn, daughter of John Hampden. Mrs Thomas's tomb can be seen at the far end of the south aisle as soon as you enter the church proper.

The present church was built in 1830-31 in replacement of one demolished in 1829. During the 1880s, when Jerome was active on the river, Hampton Church was restored – the nave in 1885 and the sanctuary in 1888.

Chapter 8   Jerome and Harris stopped under the willows by Kempton Park and lunched. Here again, at first sight, it would seem that Jerome had been mistaken and had muddled Kempton Park with Hurst Park. Hurst Park, opposite Hampton, was towpath side, and there was a wide stretch of land back to the fence protecting what used to be Hurst Park racecourse.

A letter from Jerome in the *Lock to Lock Times* proved he had not erred. There have been certain important changes in the area since 1888. Nowadays no law-abiding person would pull up on the bank opposite Hurst Park, as it is obviously private. It is owned by Thames Water and the high bank forms the boundary of their filter beds. But

these beds and other works were not constructed until 1892, four years
after the incident related by Jerome. The spoil from these works was
used to build up Platt's Ait, now occupied by a boatyard. It will be seen
that the level of this island is considerably higher than the land on
either side of the river.

On a fine summer's day in the 1880s, hundreds of canoes, skiffs
and punts would mass on the Thames, many of them moored to
the towpath bank while their crews brewed the tea and other refreshments. In the case of Kempton Park these people would be trespassers.
No doubt the owner did not object to such use being made of his land:
the demands of the 'riverside rough' were made without the owner's
knowledge, and it appears from Jerome's letter (quoted below) and his
remarks in the book that, thanks to the laziness and timidity of the
majority of the public, it was a paying game.

> Sir,
>
> ### Blackmailing on the Thames
>
> The other Sunday I camped for lunch on the favourite bit of
> ground under the willows by Kempton Park. As is getting so
> usual now, a man came round to know if everybody knew that
> this was private ground, etc. I saw many people give him a shilling
> – he must have made some half-a-sovereign in about ten minutes.
> When he came to me I took no notice of him. He blustered a good
> deal, and I told him to go and fetch his master, and offered him
> my name and address. He went off very excited to fetch his
> master, who, he said, was only a few steps off, and he'd precious
> soon show me, etc., etc. We waited very comfortably for an hour
> but neither he nor his master came. Who was he, and what did he
> do with the money, and what would you call the people who are
> simple enough to part?
>
> Yours etc.,
> August 27, 1888   JEROME K. JEROME

In an earlier issue of the *Lock to Lock Times* another correspondent
warned of similar attempts to extort money a mile or so upstream, at
Walton. Here again a shilling was demanded, and it is interesting to
speculate whether the same man was concerned in each case.

Among other factors that should be borne in mind is that in those
days Hurst Park was known as Moulsey Hurst, and that Kempton
Park, which now relates to the racecourse, was most likely the name of
a locality: indeed, it is possible that Kempton Park then included the
land now given over to filter beds alongside the river.

One might wonder why Jerome took the trouble to trespass, even
with the owner's acquiescence, on private ground, when he could have

picnicked comfortably on the towpath opposite; and in fact why these private patches were obviously so popular with the public generally. Today there would be no good reason, but we should remember that in those days much towing took place and anyone sitting on the bank beside the towpath would have to be continually alert for, and avoid, the passing towropes.

Throughout the trip Jerome and his friends appeared to moor wherever they pleased, and usually to private property. No doubt the towpath was avoided not only because of the towing nuisance but also to ensure privacy. Their first night's mooring, 'in a pleasant nook' at Picnic Point, part of the Ankerwycke estate, and on the non-towpath side of the river, was delightfully secluded. Many riparian owners seem to have been extraordinarily benevolent in the way they allowed the public the use of their grounds along the river. Some may have tried to appropriate the backwaters, but many of them were tolerant of picnickers and campers. For instance, Mr John Foster, the owner of Hartslock Woods, near Goring, would willingly grant permission for camping and picnicking in the woods. And what is more, he conveyed his permission on a card embellished with an engraving of the premises.

There are now two locks at Sunbury: the original lock, the one nearer the Middlesex bank, which was there in the 1880s, and a new lock alongside it, which was constructed in 1925. The old lock house, the one with which Jerome would have been familiar, was demolished years ago. It was on the lock island, whereas the present house stands alongside the towpath.

The weir stream can be strong and dangerous: in the 1880s it was known as Sunbury Race. Jerome advised against rowing up it, and it will be remembered that he related the story of the time he tried to do so, when, after five minutes sculling he was exactly where he started.

Chapter 8   Walton, a place that Jerome praised for modestly hiding itself from the river, is still reticent, and it is easy to pass by without realizing that only a short distance away is a busy High Street lined with shops and stores. It is true that the half-dozen houses that Jerome noted from his boat have increased considerably, but not to such an extent as to give the appearance of a bustling town.

Jerome says that Caesar had some connection with Walton. It is alleged that he crossed the river just above the site of Walton bridge, and that Cassivellaunus, who was opposing him, attempted to delay Caesar's crossing by studding the bed of the river with large wooden stakes. Hence Coway Stakes, the present name of the area. Jerome called it Corway Stakes. It is rumoured that years ago, when river work was being carried out here, some huge baulks of timber were found embedded. A more recent find, taken from the bed of the river four hundred yards below Walton bridge, was a dug-out canoe, about eighteen feet long.

St Mary's Church, Walton, unlike Hampton Church, is well away from the river, and you will not even see the top of the tower when passing in a boat. The iron Scold's Bridle in Walton Church, mentioned by Jerome, remained there until it was stolen in 1965. On my visit to the church I happened to meet the wife of a former verger, who told me the story of how her husband had years ago painstakingly made a replica of the bridle, on finding that the original was disintegrating with age, and, thanks to his skill and enthusiasm, this was able to take the place of the original after the theft.

Thus it is a replica which can now been seen inside the glass-fronted case which housed the original for so many years. On the door of the cabinet is a brass plate inscribed with the following couplet:

> Chester presents Walton with a bridle,
> to curb women's tongues that talk too idle

The cabinet would have been seen by Jerome, for an inscription informs us that it was presented in 1884.

Queen Elizabeth I visited Walton, we are told by Jerome, and he continues 'You can never get away from that woman, go where you will. She was nuts on public-houses, was England's virgin queen.' Her visits to churches were rarer, or perhaps less publicised, for it seems strange to read in the church guide that Queen Elizabeth, when at a service in Walton Church, composed the following rhyme:

> Christ was the word and spake it,
> He took the bread and brake it,
> And what the work doth make it,
> That I believe and take it.

At the time Queen Elizabeth was residing at Oatlands Palace.

Chapter 8

Several houses occupied the site of the palace successively, until in 1856 the then existing house was remodelled and extended and Oatlands Park Hotel came into existence. The hotel still flourishes, and it is difficult to imagine a more imposing setting: it is surrounded by spacious and well maintained grounds, which retain an aura of their distinguished history.

The dogs' cemetery mentioned by Jerome was established by a former Duchess of York when she lived at Oatlands. She was the wife of the man who achieved fame by marching his men to the top of the hill and marching them down again. The Duchess died in 1820.

Although I knew there was an hotel at Oatlands I was not sure whether the dogs' cemetery still existed. It could have been blotted out by a new housing estate or some other development. In the early '60s I telephoned the secretary at the hotel and was told that the cemetery was still there in a corner of the grounds. She willingly gave me permission to visit it, and I arrived there one sunny autumn day. Fine trees are scattered among the lawns between the entrance gates and the hotel. Walking through a rose garden and by a golf course I found the copse that hid the small gravestones (*Plate 3*).

I imagined that this quiet spot was rarely visited, even by the hotel guests. Nobody came to it during the two hours I was there, and the stream of golfers putting on the nearby green paid me no attention, even if they could see me in the shade of the trees. Hidden in the grove of trees the gravestones were set along footpaths, and in what may be called the central area was a large memorial stone with the following inscription:

Faithful Queenie
MDCCCLXXI

Set around this stone, in a semi-circle were about twenty-five smaller stones, some of comparatively recent date. Below are some examples of the inscriptions:

In memory of darling Becky
10th June 1931

. . .

Petite Cartouche

. . .

Dinah

A faithfuly companion
Died much respected
22 June 1881 aged 7 years

. . .

Mab

Aged 15 years
1889

Some, possibly the older graves, had only a name:

Princess
Duchess
Crafty
Fox
Romer
Cora
Ginger
Fritz

There were one or two cats:

Tiddlywinks
a beautiful tabby
died 23 August 1930
aged 11 years 2 months

Then simply

Jim
a black cat

Altogether there were about sixty-nine graves.

In 1973 the gravestones were removed and the site levelled to make way for a housing estate.

The grotto, which did not impress Jerome, stood alongside the dogs' cemetery until it was demolished in 1948. It was built about 1788 and was thus a century old when he visited it. There were two floors, and the total area covered by the grotto was about 70 feet by 40 feet. The upper chamber, which in its later years suffered damage by vandals, was, possibly because it overlooked her pets' graves, a favourite retreat of the Duchess of York. The two ramps leading to it were studded with horses' teeth, reputedly collected on the field of Waterloo.

The lower floor had a gaming room, a central room with its roof a mass of stalactites, and a room with a bath 10 feet 9 inches long and 15 feet wide. This lower floor was comparatively undamaged, and it is sad that it was not preserved. It is due to the energy and enthusiasm of Mr J.W. Lindus Forge, an architect, that a full description exists of the grotto just before its destruction.

Charles Dickens Junior in his *Dictionary of the Thames* for 1882 seems to have agreed with Jerome that there was not much to see in the grotto.

> The famous grotto, which took 20 years to construct and upon which no less than £40,000 is said to have been wasted, still exists, and is shown to visitors for a small fee. How £40,000 could have been spent in constructing two or three rooms and a passage of oyster-shells and cement is a mystery.

Among the many distinguished visitors to the grotto, were Horace Walpole in 1788, and Queen Victoria in 1871. The Queen also viewed the little cemetery with sympathy and interest and she suggested that it should be restored.

Although the very solid structure of the grotto existed until as recently as 1948, there is now no trace of it.

Joseph Farington, the Royal Academician, whose diaries were discovered in 1921, is known for his aquatint illustrations to Boydell's

History of the Thames, which was published in 1793. Like his fellow
diarist, Samuel Pepys, he seems to have known every important person
of his time. He visited the grotto at Oatlands and described it in detail.
Possibly because he saw it in its prime, Farington was favourably
impressed.

> The Duke of Newcastle had a grotto made which is much
> admired for the beauty of the workmanship and exactness of the
> imitation. Before it is a small basin of water. The whole is
> enclosed by trees which make the situation secluded. The grotto
> contains 2 small rooms, and a bathing room on the ground floor
> besides passages, and one large room above. All finished in
> character, with imitations of Icicles, and Shell work. The stones
> of which the grotto is composed were brought from Bath and
> Cirencester. The Spar of which the Icicles are composed, from
> Derbyshire. The whole was put together by a man of the name of
> Lane and his son. They were common masons by trade and lived
> at Westbury in Wiltshire. They were constantly employed six
> years about it. The Duchess of York in the course of last summer
> (1783) breakfasted and dined in the Grotto very often.

Here, perhaps, are some clues to the problem posed by Dickens:
how could so large a sum be spent on such a small structure? To import
stone from distant parts of the country would have been expensive
and, even with the low wages of those days, the employment of two
skilled men for six years would account for a tidy sum. Whether it was
worth it was another matter.

The dogs' cemetery was started a few years after Farington's visit,
but the Duchess's love of animals had not passed unnoticed, as you will
see from the following entry for 8th June 1794:

> A fire happened at Oatlands yesterday which damaged some of
> the art buildings. The King had been there, and brought back a
> little dog belonging to the Duchess of York, who seemed more
> anxious about her animals than about the House. She has 18
> dogs. The King observed that affection must rest on something.
> When there were no children animals were the object of it.

No doubt some of these eighteen dogs, which could claim acquaintance with Royalty, were among the first denizens of the little cemetery
set in the quiet dell at Oatlands.

Oatlands is set on rising ground near the Thames; the roof of the
building can be seen from both the old river and the new channel
between Walton and Shepperton. It will be remembered that Jerome
complained that above Walton bridge the river winds tremendously.
'This makes it look picturesque' he says, 'but it irritates you from a
towing or sculling point of view, and causes argument between the

man who is pulling and the man who is steering.' About forty years after Jerome wrote this the Thames Conservancy did something about it. They dug a channel that bypasses the river's meanderings. It leaves the old river just by Coway Stakes and runs for three-quarters of a mile to rejoin the main stream immediately below D'Oyly Carte Island. This channel, which was named the Desborough Channel after Lord Desborough, who was for many years Chairman of the Thames Conservancy, was constructed between 1930 and 1934. It is 100 feet wide and 10 feet deep. It must be admitted they did not dig the channel to aid scullers or towers – it was for the relief of flooding.

The old river, thus by-passed, is quiet and peaceful. If you are not in a hurry it is worth taking this route, if only to see the villages of Halliford and Shepperton, which are still 'both pretty little spots where they touch the river'. Shepperton church is near the river, and it will be remembered that Jerome, fearing that the temptation to see, in the churchyard, the tomb with a poem on it would be too strong for Harris, diverted his attention by jerking his cap into the water.

Chapter 8

In this story Jerome proves that he had an intimate knowledge of the river and riverside places, for any casual visitor to St Nicholas's church, Shepperton, would look in vain for the grave. The one referred to by Jerome is out of sight round the tower: it is a solitary tomb and a sad one, for it records in verse the death of a little girl, the daughter of the poet, Thomas Love Peacock (*Plate 22*). The inscription and poem are easily read on the weathered stone:

MARGARET LOVE PEACOCK
Born March 25th 1823
Died January 13th 1826

Long night succeeds thy little day,
Oh blighted blossom can it be
That this grey stone and grassy clay
Have closed our anxious care of thee?

The half-formed words of liveliest thought
That spoke a mind beyond thy years
The song, the dance by nature taught
The sunny smiles: the transient tears.

The symmetry of face and form
The eye with light and life replete
The little heart so fondly warm
The voice so musically sweet.

These, lost to hope, in memory yet
Around the hearts that loved thee cling
Shadowing with long and vain regret
The too fair promise of thy spring.

Who could stand by this grave and read this poem without feeling sad? Perhaps Jerome was not so hard-hearted as he pretended. No doubt he had seen the grave on a previous visit and we can guess that on the trip with Harris he did not wish to be saddened by the reminder of the death of this little girl.

Thomas Love Peacock lived beside the Thames for many years, and his favourite riverside house at Halliford still exists. He died in 1866. His grave, in Shepperton Cemetery, is scarcely a hundred yards from that of his little daughter, who died forty years before him.

Chapter 8   The River Wey, 'a pretty little stream, navigable for small boats up to Guildford', joins the Thames just below Shepperton Lock. Jerome tells us that he had always been trying to make up his mind to explore this river, and never had. This is true today of many river men, who are determined that one day they will leave the Thames and tour the Wey: but they never seem to do it. For many years the River Wey was a private company, but it then was taken over by the National Trust.

Jerome and Harris met up with George at Shepperton Lock. The lock-keeper, who heard all the commotion of their arrival and rushed out with a drag under the impression that somebody had fallen into the lock, was Mr W. Smith. He himself was drowned in November 1890.

The towpath ends on the Surrey bank just below the lock and continues on the opposite bank. At that time a ferry connected the towpath at this point; after some years of closure when the towpath rambler had no means of crossing the river here, it was pleasing to see in 1993 that a regular ferry service had been re-introduced.

The lock has been rebuilt since Jerome's journey: the lock-keeper's house, which was near the top of the lock, was demolished by a bomb in World War II. The lock is beside the road, and it is still a convenient place to meet your friends. To reach the station, which is over a mile away, you walk through old Shepperton and past the church square. They could have saved George a long walk if they had arranged to meet him at the public wharf near the square, but Jerome would then not have been able to prevent Harris from visiting a little girl's grave with a poem on it.

Chapter 9   George, who had just joined the party, towed the boat, somewhat reluctantly, from Shepperton Lock to Penton Hook. Bungalows and houses now line much of this stretch of river, though some open country remains. Jerome, Harris and George would have seen few riverside buildings, except at Chertsey and Laleham. By Chertsey bridge, on the Surrey shore, the Bridge House Hotel, which was known to all river men in the '80s, still exists. The bridge, which replaced an earlier one, was built between 1780 and 1785. When Jerome and his party passed through Chertsey lock on the trip, it was of wooden construction. The present lock was built in 1913.

Penton Hook lock has also been rebuilt since the days of *Three Men in a Boat*, but the main part of the lock-house is original, as will be seen from the City of London crest and the date on its facade. It was here that the party, after discussion, decided to push on for Runnymede, and the gallant George, who had already towed the laden boat the four miles from Shepperton lock, proceeded to haul it for nearly two more to Staines Bridge. They would have crossed the river at Staines railway bridge, where the towpath changes sides, and then Jerome and Harris shared the towing until they reached Bell Weir Lock.

They had decided to spend their first night near Magna Carta Island, about a mile above Bell Weir Lock. They soon regretted this decision, and found the long pull from Penton Hook Lock exhausting at the end of a strenuous day. As Jerome said, 'A bit of water between a coal-barge and a gasworks would have quite satisfied us for that night.' It is likely that in his reference to coal barges and gasworks Jerome had in mind the gasworks, with wharf alongside, that they would have passed on the right bank a short distance upstream of Staines Bridge. At this point they would have been feeling tired, as they looked ahead hope-fully for Bell Weir Lock. Chapter 10

In his reconstruction of Magna Carta, Jerome tells us that the night before this great event King John slept at Duncroft Hall. The present Duncroft Hall is just across the road from St Mary's church at Staines, and within sight of the London (City) Stone, which stands beside the Thames. Jerome imagined the King's cavalcade riding along the road from Staines and embarking on the barges to be ferried to the island now known as Magna Carta Island. He (Jerome) referred to the argu-ment that persists to this day, and will never end, as to whether the historic event took place on Runnymede itself or on the island. Chapter 11

If the King's party did indeed ride along the road from Staines they would have crosed the Thames by the old Roman bridge, which spanned the river about 100 yards below the present bridge.

The Roman name for Staines, *Ad Pontes*, indicated that there was more than one bridge at Staines; in addition to the Thames bridge there would have been a bridge over the River Colne, a small fast-flowing tributary, which joins the main stream just above the site of the Roman bridge. Staines is now a busy town; in earlier days it would have been a cluster of houses around the church and near the bridge. The majority of the old houses remaining in Staines are in this area, particu-larly Church Street, leading from the bridge to the church.

Magna Carta Island is not far away, and it would have taken King John and his entourage only a few minutes to ride to where the barges were waiting to take them across the river.

The Three Men had intended to go on to Magna Carta Island, but pulled up at Picnic Point 'and dropped into a very pleasant nook under a great elm tree'. Picnic Point, a prominent river feature, is about 400 yards below Magna Carta Island. It forms part of the Ankerwycke

Estate, which is owned by the County Council. Many fine trees, notably chestnuts, overhang this site (*Plate 14*).

Picnic Point is believed to have got its name from a small thatched cottage, known as the Picnic, which stood on the river's edge a short distance upstream. The cottage was burnt down in the 1940s: the occupant, a recluse, lost his life in the fire.

Ankerwycke Estate was in those days privately owned. No doubt the owner did not object to people tying up to his bank, provided they behaved themselves. In contrast, now that the Estate is owned by Berks County Council, the public are not allowed to moor overnight. Just beside the probable mooring spot is now a notice warning the public that night mooring is not allowed. No doubt Jerome and Harris – particularly Harris – would have known what to do with the notice board. One imagines Harris setting fire to the County Council offices, and singing a comic song on the ruins. (*Plate 13*).

On the opposite shore stretches Runnymede, with the wooded slopes of Coopers Hill behind. Very little will have changed since the 1880s. The road still runs beside the river on the Surrey side, though it is a new and wider road, built to serve the motor car. The RAF Memorial on top of the hill is new: the other two memorials, the American Bar Association Memorial, a temple-like structure commemorating Magna Carta, and the more recent Kennedy Memorial, are tucked away and not easily seen. If the Three Men were to return to their mooring at Picnic Point they would feel completely at home in familiar surroundings; but no doubt they would comment upon the noise of the cars on the other side of the river, and the roar of the jets from Heathrow Airport.

In the forbidden grounds of Ankerwycke the ruins of the old priory are hidden amidst the trees; if you wish to see them or to walk the ground on which Henry VIII courted Anne Boleyn, you will have to trespass. The other local historic spot visited by Jerome and his companions, Magna Carta Island, with the small cottage containing the stone on which the Carta is said to have been signed, or sealed, is also owned by the County Council. The property is let on a long lease to a private individual, and it appears that no provision is made for the public to see the site.

The Ankerwycke shore between the mooring at Picnic Point and Magna Carta Island is today exactly as it always has been. Large chestnuts and sycamores line the bank. Among the smaller shrubs are numerous clumps of wild honeysuckle. If they were there in the 1880s, they presumably gladdened Jerome's heart, for it will be remembered that in the story of the Datchet hotels he rejected the first because there was no honeysuckle about the porch.

Jerome gives no fewer than 38 pages to the description of incidents at this, their first mooring place on the holiday. The putting up of the

Chapter 7

Chapter 10

Chapter 11

Chapter 12

Chapter 10

canvas, their first meal, the disturbed night, and Jerome's involuntary swim next morning, would naturally loom large. For the following and subsequent nights such events would be routine. But when full allowance is made for that aspect, Jerome visualizing in his mind's eye their mooring in the 'soft green valley' was no doubt influenced by the pleasant memories of a happy evening, and by the historic associations of the spot: for surely, in the whole length of the upper Thames you will not find so much history crammed into so small an area.

The *Lock to Lock Times* for 1888 gave a clue to the public when it reported that great changes were taking place in Datchet and that the construction of new roads was proceeding apace. Today Datchet has the distinction of having two level-crossings within 100 yards of each other. The one that now leads directly from the river to the village and which brings you to the Manor Hotel, was not in existence during the years that Jerome was making his river trips. The road was a cul-de-sac leading to and ending at the station. So the only way they could reach the village would be by the other level-crossing, and by this route they could cross the main road, and reach the Stag first.

The two hotels still flourish; the Manor Hotel is considerably larger than the Royal Stag (to give it its full name). The latter hotel is painted cream, and is unusual in that it is built into the local churchyard. The church itself has a financial interest in the pub and a proportion of the takings go to the church funds. It could be said that the spoils are divided between God and Mammon.

From Datchet, Jerome and his part towed steadily on, to a little below Monkey Island. They passed through Windsor on the way, but he makes no mention of it. The larger and better known riverside towns fare badly in *Three Men in a Boat*: like the true river man he was, Jerome preferred to dwell on the little secret and deserted spots, such as their mooring places at Picnic Point and among the Shiplake Islands.

In *Three Men in a Boat*, Monkey Island is connected with the sad occasion that the Three Men found themselves without mustard, and their gloom was intensified by their abortive attempts to open a tin of pineapples. Monkey Island does not really deserve to be associated with such calamity, for it is a pleasant spot and for many years, first as an inn and now as an hotel, it has served the public. Dickens' *Dictionary of the Thames* tells us that in the 1880s it was used by anglers, oarsmen and camping parties. The island is separated from the right bank by a small backwater and the towpath runs on the other (Bucks) bank. No doubt Jerome's party moored to the well wooded bank below the island.

According to some authorities Monkey Island is so called because of the pictures of monkeys that adorn the walls and ceiling of a room in the hotel. These charming pictures date from the time that the building was a fishing lodge owned by the Duke of Marlborough in the early

Chapter 12

eighteenth century. However it seems the pictures may have been painted in reference to an already existing name, which may have derived from a community of monks on the island in medieval times.

Some pleasant modern houses are set back in their gardens on the Bucks side, but the area in many ways is little different from in the 1880s, although there is, sadly, the constant background roar of M4 traffic which crosses the river a few hundred yards upsteam.

In 1887 the proprietor of Monkey Island Hotel, P. Plummer, was advertising 'a good hot ordinary always ready between one and three on Sundays at one and sixpence a head'. As this advertisement appeared in *Fishing*, a weekly magazine, it was presumably addressed to anglers; but boating parties were also welcomed.

Chapter 12   Jerome was not fond of Maidenhead, nor did he admire the type of people who were to be found there – 'the river swell and his overdressed female companion'. He and his party hurried through Maidenhead to Boulter's Lock. This lock, which was then in its heyday, was one of the most popular spots on the Thames, and on Ascot Sunday one of the most populous. The then lock-keeper, W.H. Turner, was a well known character, noted for the efficient way he sped the massed craft through his lock, aided by several assistants. Boulter's lock was reconstructed and enlarged in 1909 (*Plates 5 and 6*).

Once they were through Boulter's lock the party took their time passing through Cliveden reach. In those days it was generally spelt Clieveden. A mansion, the third on the site, is perched on the top of the wooded hill, and is now the property of the National Trust.

Jerome bestows some of his superlatives on this stretch of river. Little will have changed in the intervening years: as you travel upstream and catch the first glimpse of Cliveden House, with the woods, river and islands below you can be certain that this is exactly what Jerome and his companions saw – no more, no less.

They had tea in the backwater just below Cookham, and presumably this was in the weir stream, which runs parallel to the lock cut. The lock was enlarged in 1892 and reconstructed in 1956. The lock may be different, but almost everything else in sight is the same as 100 years ago. The wooded heights of Cliveden tower over the lock, and, apart from the lock-house, there is not a building in sight. At the side of My Lady Ferry, a few hundred yards below the lock, the towpath crosses the river to the Bucks bank, and it used to pass, with the aid of two more ferries, to the Berkshire shore just by Cookham bridge. It is sad that none of these ferries is now working, for in this lovely stretch of river to walk first on one bank and then on the other, with short voyages in between, must have been delightful. Nowadays only the boating man or woman can enjoy the full pleasures of this reach. The pedestrian must make a detour inland when he reaches My Lady Ferry site. Although he has to depart from the river and miss some of the glory of Cliveden heights, he will be consoled by a pleasant walk along a shady lane until he reaches the outskirts of Cookham. A narrow path that runs between the bridge and Turk's boathouse leads to the tow-path. Like its relative downstream at Kingston, Turk's boathouse is a wooden structure that dates from before the days of *Three Men in a Boat*.

Once through Cookham lock, it will be recalled, the party took advantage of the unexpectedly favourable breeze and hoisted the sail. In those days many river craft were provided with large keels or centre-boards, and consequently they would have lacked manoeuvrability. The lug-sail would easily block the view of the helmsman, and in the circumstances it is not surprising they went slap into the punt of the three irate fishermen.

Chapter 12

After their accident George steered the boat and brought them up to Marlow. They would appear to have sailed all the way, and what a delightful sail it must have been; for the first two miles the country on either side is flat and open, and then, as you approach Marlow, Winter Hill and Quarry Woods meet the river.

Jerome was fond of Marlow. He described it as a bustling, lively little town, and as one of the pleasantest river centres he knew of. This description is true of the present town. In common with other popular riverside places such as Henley and Abingdon, Marlow, in some magic way, retains a Victorian air, in spite of much new building. It is because this air is impossible to define or capture that these rare places are in great danger today. That they have survived so long is due less to design than to accident. A wrong decision by a planning committee can destroy this very fragile thing; and who, with any experience of planners and their ways, would rely upon their always making the right decision? The Thames is so much more than a beautiful waterway: it is a channel connecting the past with the present. One of its great attractions to anyone who knows and loves it is that at unexpected moments it can transport us back to the days of our great-grandparents.

Chapter 13

That Jerome himself experienced this particular kind of magic there can be no doubt. Writing about Quarry Woods on the outskirts of Marlow he says, 'Dear old Quarry Woods! with your narrow climbing paths, and little winding glades, how scented to this hour you seem with memories of sunny summer days! How haunted are your shadowy vistas with the ghosts of laughing faces! How from your whispering leaves there softly fall the voices of long ago!' (*Back cover*)

It is easy to imagine that not one leaf nor one tree has changed in Quarry Woods since those words were written. You can walk the narrow climbing paths and obtain occasional glimpses of the river far below. It is true there are buildings in the woods, some of which are modern, but they are hidden among the trees. In the 1880s there was a scare about extensive building in the woods, as will be seen in the following extract from the *Lock to Lock Times* of 23rd June 1888:-

> . . . today it is my painful duty to announce the impending spoila-
> tion of one of the most beautiful spots on the Upper Thames.
> Comment is needless: the fact will appeal to all real lovers of our
> river – Quarry Woods are doomed. The details are already deter-
> mined on. Quarry Woods is to become a title of the past, and in
> its place we are to have the "Bisham Building Estate" on which a
> large number of houses are to be erected at the cost of one
> hundred thousand pounds. The first step has already been taken.
> Mr E. Vansittart Neale has already laid his plans before the
> Bisham Vestry, and has obtained their consent to the diverting of
> certain existing footpaths, and the making of a new road, and
> unless those responsible, by some untoward chance, wake up to
> the short-sightedness of the policy to which they have pledged
> themselves, nothing can save the lovely background of Marlow,
> so familiar to the rowing man and the artist.

This serious threat was averted. Quarry Woods still exists, and
much of this area is now in the safe keeping of the National Trust.

At Marlow Jerome and his companions left the boat by the bridge
and put up for the night at the Crown. The bridge at Marlow is still
there. Since it was opened in 1835 it has been a prominent part of the
Marlow river scene, and it is unusual on the upper Thames in being of
the suspension type. Recently completely reconstructed, it owes its
preservation to its appearance, for nobody could contemplate the
thought of Marlow without its suspension bridge.

The Crown, an old coaching inn, is at the top of Marlow High
Street. Mr Henry Calf was the proprietor in Jerome's time. The road is
wide between this inn and the bridge, and it is easy to imagine how
imposing was the procession as Jerome and party, accompanied by all
the shop boys loaded with provisions, walked to the river to embark in
their skiff. Turn left at the Crown and you will find yourself in West
Street, where, Jerome tells us, Shelley was living when he composed
'The Revolt of Islam'. If you look carefully you will see the plaque that
marks his house.

Bisham Abbey, which Jerome tells us was the home of Anne of
Cleves and of Queen Elizabeth, now houses the National Sports
Centre. On its immaculate lawns students rest from their exertions,
and good use is made of the river by those learning to canoe or sail. Just
downstream overlooking the river is Bisham Church of which Jerome
says, 'if any tombs are worth inspecting, they are the tombs and monuments in Bisham Church.' Praise indeed from one who on the journey
upstream had done everything he could to prevent Harris from making
just such an inspection.

Hurley Weir, which was also praised by Jerome, retains its charm and indeed is now equipped with a salmon ladder, but the outskirts of Hurley have been spoilt by various caravan sites. On Danes' Field, where, Jerome tells us, the invading Danes once encamped, you will now see a host of caravans. The Three, who could even now travel from Windsor to Marlow and from Medmenham upstream without being unduly disturbed, would not be happy about what has happened at Hurley.

We do not know whether they sculled or towed the boat up river when they set off from Marlow. It is likely they towed, for it will be remembered that the skiff was heavily laden with their purchases at Marlow: according to Bacon's *Guide* 'towing' pays 'better than rowing, if the stream is at all strong or the boat heavy'. From Marlow the towpath runs on the left bank to Temple Lock, and in Jerome's day a ferry just above the lock connected with the continuation of the path on the Berks shore. At Hurley the towpath crossed the lower lock cut by means of a footbridge and returned to Berkshire over a sister bridge spanning the upper cut. From there it skirted Danes' Field to Medmenham and crossed to the other bank by ferry. The towpath today follows the same line, but is cut into dead-end sections by the absence of ferries. However an impressive monument stands on the site of the Medmenham Ferry, commemorating legal action taken by Viscount Devenport in 1899 to establish the public right to use it. Chapter 13

Even if they did tow, they occasionally got aboard and pushed out into mid-stream whenever they saw a steam launch approaching. Jerome boasted that their one small boat, during that week, 'caused more annoyance and delay and aggravation to the steam-launches that we came across than all the other craft on the river put together.'

Medmenham Abbey has changed little, and the village, which is hidden from the river, is quiet and peaceful.

'From Medmenham to sweet Hambledon Lock the river is full of peaceful beauty,' Jerome tells us. Hambleden was spelt -don in those days. It is pleasant to be able to record that the spelling is the only thing that has changed, for surely no stretch of country could be less affected by the twentieth century.

At Hambleden Lock, it will be remembered, George asked the lock-keeper for some water, and was told to take as much as he wanted and to leave the rest. The lock-keeper there at the time was C. Phyllis, and he met his end when he was accidentally drowned in the lock in 1890. It is a tragic coincidence that the lock-keeper the Three Men met at Shepperton – the one who came rushing out with the drag on hearing the commotion of their arrival – was also drowned in the river in 1890.

'Greenlands, the rather uninteresting looking river residence of my newsagent' is on the left bank above Hambleden Lock. Mr W.H. Smith – the newsagent – was founder of the well known bookshop firm and prominent in politics. Jerome's description of the house is still accurate if by 'uninteresting' he means featureless, but it is a large Chapter 13 house in well kept grounds. In common with many other large river-side houses, Greenlands is no longer a private dwelling (*Plate 8*).

Henley, Jerome passes without comment, although he does mention it briefly later on. In general he avoids mention of the main tourist towns: Windsor might not have existed for all the notice it gets, and all we hear of Maidenhead is that it was too snobby to be pleasant, and that it harboured steam launches. These omissions, I believe, were deliberate on Jerome's part. Although, as we know, he had intended to write the story of the Thames, 'its scenery and history', there were, even then, scores of books which dealt with what we might call the conventional guide-book features of the river. He determined to write something different, and although he strayed in certain ways from his original intentions, 'something different' he certainly wrote.

'We went up the backwater to Wargrave,' said Jerome. This was Hennerton backwater, which is still navigable in small boats. Half-way up this backwater the party stopped for lunch: and Harris, who was carving the steak and kidney pie, disappeared when Jerome and George turned round to reach out for a spoon.

Chapter 14   When you rejoin the main stream you will find yourself on the outskirts of Wargrave. 'Wargrave, nestling where the river bends, makes a sweet old picture as you pass it.' This comment, as with so many others in *Three Men in a Boat*, is fortunately still true. It also illustrates Jerome's eye for detail, for the river certainly bends at Wargrave. Looking from the George & Dragon, Shiplake Lock on the left and Shiplake Station on the right, although only two thirds of a mile apart, are separated by more than twice that length of river.

The inn sign, described by Jerome, at the George & Dragon, had the unusual distinction of being the result of a collaboration between two Royal Academicians, G.D. Leslie and J.E. Hodgson. Leslie tells us about it in his book *Our River*, which was published in 1881.

> I painted my side first, a regular orthodox St George on a white horse, spearing the dragon. Hodgson was so taken with the idea of painting a signboard that he asked me to be allowed to do the other side, to which I, of course, consented, and as he could only stop at Wargrave one day he managed to do it on that day; indeed it occupied him little more than a couple of hours. The idea of his composition was suggested by Signor Pellegrini, the well-known artist of *Vanity Fair*; the picture represented St George, having vanquished the dragon, and dismounted from his horse, quenching his thirst in a large beaker of ale. These pictures were duly hung up soon after and very much admired; they have since had a coat of boat varnish, and look already very old masterly. Hodgson's, which gets the sun on it, is a little faded, but mine, which faces the north, towards Henley, still looks pretty fresh.

The *Lock to Lock Times* of 30th June 1888 reported that the sign-board had been taken down and was reposing in the boathouse. 'It is worn, cracked and quite "old-masterish" in appearance. Mr Leslie has promised to renovate it, and it will soon be creaking again in the breeze.'

You can see the signboard today, recently restored, in the George & Dragon. Plans are afoot to hang a replica outside the pub, now a Harvester Inn, so once again St George will stand in his rightful place proclaiming both his victory and the name of the pub to the outside world, while it is good to know that the original painting is carefully preserved inside (*Plate 25*).

The church at Wargrave is well tucked away and not easy to find. When eventually I found it my efforts were rewarded, for the church is in a superb setting, standing at the far end of a green and surrounded on three sides by fine mature trees.

I searched the church for the memorial to Mrs Sarah Hill mentioned by Jerome. This was not an easy task, for some of the tablets are set high on the walls and the light was poor. In spite of a thorough search I could not find the memorial: when I read the church guide I got a hint as to what might have happened, for in 1914 the building was practically destroyed by fire. There can be little doubt that the tablet was lost at that time. But although the tablet has gone, the Sarah Hill Benefaction continued at least until the 1960s; every year four pupils at the Junior School were given four shillings each.

From Wargrave and past Shiplake the Three appeared to have **Chapter 14** sailed, for we read that they caught a breeze after lunch and that took them past these places. Jerome reported that the river between Shiplake and Sonning was very placid, hushed and lonely, and that few folk walk along its banks. This is an accurate description of this reach today: the towpath runs on the left bank, and the few people who follow it on foot for the three miles between the two delightful villages see little sign of life other than the numerous cattle in the meadows. What is more, the houses they pass – confined to a small cluster at the top of the St Patrick's Stream – are charming, and in no way detract from the beauty of the reach.

Many years ago at a London Livery Company dinner I met Mr Frank Carr, who was then the Director of the Maritime Museum at Greenwich. We found that we had a mutual love of the Thames; and during our talk he told me that his two favourite books were *Three Men in a Boat* and *The Riddle of the Sands* by Erskine Childers. I have talked about the former with many fellow enthusiasts but Mr Carr displayed more interest than most in the topographical details that have intrigued me for years. A simple question, 'Do you know which of the islands at Shiplake Jerome's party moored to?' was sufficient to start a lengthy discussion.

As it happened I had spent some time at Shiplake during the previous

summer trying to identify the island. It will be remembered that
Jerome and George had left Harris and Montmorency in the boat,
which was moored to one of the islands, while they walked to Henley
and spent the evening with friends. Rain was falling when they set out
to walk the four miles back to the boat, and when they arrived there, at
about midnight, they could not remember which of the islands the boat
was moored to. In reply to Jerome's question, George said that there
were four islands.

There are still four islands, though the fourth is separated by only a
narrow channel from the Oxfordshire bank. The towpath from Shiplake
runs on this bank. The first island, going upstream, which is the way
that the two companions were walking, is small and compact, in the
centre of the river. It is called Phillimore's Island. The second, The
Lynch, about a furlong upstream, is larger and less well defined. The
third, the largest, and known as Hallsmead Ait, is well wooded, and the
fourth, Buck Ait, as already indicated, can scarcely be considered an
island. Even in the 1880s it is doubtful whether it would have been
possible to float a skiff in the channel on the towpath side.

Chapter 14 Jerome says, 'We despairingly tried what seemed in the darkness to
be the fourth island, but met with no better success.' They then caught
sight, a little way below them, of a 'weird sort of glimmer flickering
amongst the trees', which came from the boat. This would indicate that
the boat was moored to the third island. They were looking downstream
from the fourth, and the second is hidden around a sharp bend and
would not have been visible. We should remember that the party were
at Sonning when they decided to go back to one of the Shiplake Islands
for the night. It is reasonable to assume that they would not go further
downstream than necessary, and the third island would, from many
points of view, be the first reasonable island site.

We shall never know for sure which of the islands it was. But, having
given further consideration to all the points, I would still give the
answer I gave to Mr Carr – 'The third island' (*Plate 18*).

I surmised that Jerome used certain guide books and maps when
writing *Three Men in a Boat*. However well he might have known the
river he would need occasionally to jog his memory about details. One
of the maps he consulted was the *Oarsman's and Angler's Map of the
River Thames*. Though this map shows various islands at Shiplake they
are not sufficiently well defined to indicate the island of the 'swans'
incident. A much better map from this aspect is *A Bird's eye View of the
Thames*, published about the same date as the other map, which shows
clearly the four islands.

Chapter 14 Sonning is described as 'the most fairy-like little nook on the whole
river. It is more like a stage village than one built of bricks and mortar.
Every house is smothered in roses, and now, in early June, they were
bursting forth in clouds of dainty splendour.' The roses are still there,

the houses remain, and Sonning is still a delightful village (*Plate 23*).

Jerome tells us 'If you stop at Sonning, put up at the "Bull", behind . . . the church. It is a veritable picture of an old country inn, with green square courtyard in front, where, on seats beneath the trees, the old men group of an evening to drink their ale and gossip over village politics; with low, quaint rooms and latticed windows, and awkward stairs and winding passages.' John Bright was the proprietor in those days. You walk through the churchyard and down a path to get to the river from the inn: this brings you to the towpath, with the lock on the left and Sonning bridge to the right. For many years Sonning Lock has been noted for its garden, which is ablaze with flowers throughout the summer. The garden here was worthy of comment in the 1880s, for Dickens tells us that 'the floral tastes of the lock-keeper generally make Sonning Lock very bright and gay.' This was written in 1882, when the lock-keeper was James Sadler. In addition to being a good gardener, Sadler was noted as a bee-keeper and poet. Appointed to his post at Sonning in 1845, he retired in 1885, and was succeeded by his son Michael, who was lock-keeper at the time of *Three Men in a Boat*. It is probable that Jerome had this garden in mind, among others, when he said that the Thames would not be the fairyland it is without its flower-decked locks (*Plate 17*).

There is no other village beside the Thames to compare with Sonning, though it is in danger of being spoilt by its sophistication and self-conscious prettiness. Not the least surprising thing about this village is that it is scarcely a couple of miles away from Reading, which 'does its best to spoil and sully and make hideous as much of the river as it can reach.' As soon as you leave Sonning travelling upstream you enter Dreadnought Reach – some say it ought to be called Dreadful Reach – and Reading town is in view. Jerome tempers his criticism of Reading with a little kindness – 'Even Reading . . . is good-natured enough to keep its ugly face a good deal out of sight.' This is true today; considering its size, Reading is kind to the Thames, though two high office blocks by Reading Bridge (this bridge was not there in the 1880s) make one wonder what present-day planners are up to.

The remains of the Benedictine Abbey at Reading, to which Jerome **Chapter 16** referred, can be reached by walking through Forbury Gardens. These gardens were part of the grounds of the Abbey, and were known as Forbury, or Outer, Court. The North (or River) Gate was near the present entrance facing Vastern Road.

Reading Abbey was founded in 1121. Although much of it was demolished over four hundred years ago, the existing ruins testify to the one-time importance of the Abbey.

Harris and George sculled to Reading from their overnight mooring at the Shiplake island. It had been arranged that Jerome would tow the boat from there, but it will be remembered that they met a friend who towed them behind his steam launch. Reading Lock, where they met

the friend, is now known as Caversham Lock. At that time it was com-
paratively new, having been rebuilt in 1875. The lock-keeper was a
Mrs Knight, widow of the previous lock-keeper, who was drowned in
July 1883.

The railway that Jerome tells us spoilt the Thames near Tilehurst,
still spoils it: but fortunately, his comment that from Mapledurham to
Streatley the river was glorious, is also still true.

The towpath runs on the right bank from Reading to Tilehurst until you
come to a dead-end at the site of Roebuck Ferry. This ferry, which is now
discontinued, crossed the river to the towpath on the left bank: another
ferry, about half a mile upstream, returned to the towpath on the right
bank. These ferries were usually known as the Purley Ferries. At Mapledurham Lock, which is in a splendid setting of meadow, hill and fine
green trees, much of what you see is what Jerome and his companions
saw, though the present lock-house is on the opposite side of the lock.

Most of the locks on the river are now mechanised. This means that
the large beams on the lock gates, which until recently were familiar to
all river men, have disappeared. Mechanical power has replaced manual
power: and it is no longer possible for the onlooker to assist the lock-
keeper by pushing on the beams.

The 'quaint little Swan Inn' at Pangbourne graces the river beside
Whitchurch Weir. The lock-house here would be familiar to Jerome:
most of the older lock-houses have now been rebuilt, many of them in
the late 1950s. In the case of Whitchurch lock-house it was found
possible to retain the structure and to modernise the interior.

Just above the Swan Inn is the old boat-house (now no longer used
commercially) where the party left their skiff and made their ignominious
return to London, after suffering the drenching rain on the return
journey from Oxford. The boat-house was then owned by G. Ashley.

The Three Men, who were towed by their friend's steam launch
through two locks (Mapledurham and Whitchurch) and along ten
miles of river, were cast loose a short distance above Gatehampton
Railway Bridge, and just below The Grotto at Basildon. The Grotto, a
large white house, was so called because in the grounds there was at
one time a shell-encrusted grotto, built by the previous owner, Lady
Fane (*Plate 7*).

Chapter 16 Just after Jerome took the sculls they came upon the body of the
drowned woman! She has a chapter all to herself later in this book.

About a mile above The Grotto, Streatley bridge spans the river
(*Plate 26*). Jerome does not tell us whether during their stay in the
Goring/Streatley area they slept in their boat or in a hotel. All we know
is that on the day they arrived they left their boat at the bridge and
lunched at the Bull in Streatley. The Bull, a picturesque white-painted
inn, is on the hill, facing the road that carries heavy traffic to Reading in
the east and Wallingford in the west.

The large hump of Streatley Hill overshadows the area and the view from the top is well worth the climb. From here you look down on Streatley village immediately below, the blue ribbon of the river, and on the other side the village of Goring, with its church tower a prominent feature. Much new building has taken place, some in Streatley, but more in Goring. The new houses stand out from the old, but they are not too obvious, and you feel that Jerome, assuming that he ever climbed the hill and looked over the valley, would not be unduly perturbed by the changes he would see today. I do not doubt that he did see this view, for at one time he lived on the outskirts of Ewelme, only a few miles away on the other side of the river. A man with his lively mind and inquisitive nature would not be able to live for long within sight of such an imposing hill without succumbing to the temptation to climb it.

Of the twin villages Jerome preferred Streatley, but he had a good word for Goring, including its proximity to the railway station, which he said was handy if you wished to slip off without paying your hotel bill.

The wooden bridge connecting Streatley and Goring was built in 1837: this bridge was the one used by the Three Men, and in those days the toll to cross it was one penny. At first glance you might think that the present bridge is the old structure, but you will see on closer inspection that it is of concrete. When it replaced the previous bridge in 1923 pains were taken to make the new bridge look like the old.

During their stay at Streatley (on the second evening), Jerome and George went for a walk to Wallingford, and coming home called at a little riverside inn. This was the inn that was the subject of the story of the stuffed trout that turned out to be made of plaster of Paris. Jerome does not say whether they walked by the road or the towpath; being river men it is inconceivable that they should choose a dusty road in preference to a pastoral path beside the river, and the towpath seems to be a safe bet. The only pub along this stretch of towpath is the Beetle and Wedge at Moulsford. It is an old pub, well situated beside the ferry, and to anyone who had walked downstream from Wallingford and crossed the river by ferryboat the temptation to stop for a drink would be irresistible. The first old gentleman to claim credit for catching the trout said he caught it 'just below the bridge'; Moulsford railway bridge is less than half a mile upstream. The second claimant, the local carrier, said 'I caught him just below the lock – leastways, what was the lock then . . .' This clearly referred to Wallingford Lock, about three miles upstream, and which it will be remembered was the subject of Jerome's story of the missing lock.

No further hints are given. This may be an incident imagined by Jerome – one of the few stories relating to the river not based on fact. But it is reasonable to suppose that, even if it did not actually occur, he had in mind the Beetle and Wedge when he located the

Chapter 17

story in a little riverside inn between Wallingford and Streatley.

Jerome confessed that he was not a good fisherman due, it was alleged by his friends, to his lack of imagination. As he does not give any indication of his ever having fished during his river holidays we may assume that he was not a fisherman at all, and that he was therefore able to view the activities of anglers with cynical detachment.

In the story of the stuffed fish we read that Jim Bates claimed that the trout weighed 18 pounds 6 ounces, Joe Muggles that it weighed 26 pounds, and Billy Maunders that it scaled 34 pounds. The record for a Thames trout is not certain, but Yarrell records one of 15 pounds in 1835.

Chapter 18　　'The river is not extraordinarily interesting between Streatley and Wallingford,' said Jerome, and in this, as in so much else, he was right. He implied that this was due to the absence of locks, there being six and a half miles of clear river between Cleeve and Benson locks. This remains the longest uninterrupted stretch between locks, and, as might be expected, it is popular with the rowing man.

Jerome was not fond of the lock-keepers, many of whom, he alleged, were excitable, nervous old men, quite unfitted for their posts. He liked the flower-decked locks, however. There was a tradition of gardening at the Thames locks; the Thames Conservancy always encouraged the cultivation of the gardens.

Talking of locks reminded Jerome and George of the incident at Molesey Lock, when a speculative photographer was taking a photograph of the lock full of boats. Such an incident is unlikely nowadays, when everyone takes photographs, but in those early days, when the camera itself was a formidable piece of equipment, and having one's photograph taken was an event, it could easily have happened. Many of the river photographs of those days show the masses of craft and crowds of people, all well aware that the photographer was operating. A little inattention when the lock was filling could easily result in an accident. Even today a boat can be hung up on the side of a lock or hooked under a beam if the crew do not attend to it, but as most of them are larger, powered craft, the chance of a serious accident happening is not so likely.

The story of the missing lock at Wallingford proves that Jerome was well acquainted with the small changes that had taken place along the river in the early 1880s. It will be remembered that he was rowing his girl cousin downstream to Goring, and that they became increasingly anxious as they continued for mile after mile without reaching the lock.

Wallingford Lock was built in 1838 to ease navigation past shallows. The fall of the weir was seldom more than 20 inches, and as early as 1865 the works were in a bad state. For the next fifteen years the Thames Conservancy were unable to decide whether to demolish the lock and weir or whether to rebuild it at a cost estimated at £2,000.

There was no lack of advice and exhortation. Boating men resented paying toll at a practically non-existent lock, and the inhabitants of Wallingford, just upstream, petitioned against the removal of the lock: some doctors feared that the lowering of the water would cause epidemics in the town. The lock was removed in 1883. Jerome's abortive search for it would appear, therefore, to have been in about 1884.

Wallingford, a busy little town, retains a hint of the 1880s, perhaps because it is away from the main railway line. 'From Wallingford to Dorchester the neighbourhood of the river grows more hilly, varied and picturesque', we are told by Jerome. The most prominent hill features are, of course, Wittenham Clumps, which overhang the river by Day's Lock. Dorchester is not strictly a Thames-side town. In *Three Men in a Boat* it is stated that it can be reached by paddling up the Thames. This is a printer's error – it should be the *Thame*, a tributary that flows through Dorchester before joining the Thames about half a mile away. The walk across the fields from Day's Lock to Dorchester, as suggested by Jerome, is still pleasant and pastoral.

Chapter 18

The 'Barley Mow' inn at Clifton Hampden gets high praise from Jerome. In appearance it is much the same as when visited by him and it is easy to believe that several hundred years ago it looked much as it does now. It is deservedly a popular inn, and part of its popularity may still be due to Jerome's recommendation:

> Round Clifton Hampden, itself a wonderfully pretty village, old-fashioned, peaceful and dainty with flowers, the river scenery is rich and beautiful. If you stay the night on land at Clifton, you cannot do better than put up at the Barley Mow. It is, without exception, I should say, the quaintest, most old-world inn up the river. It stands on the right of the bridge, quite away from the village. Its low-pitched gable and thatched roof and latticed windows give it quite a story-book appearance, while inside it is even still more once-upon-a-timeyfied.
>
> It would not be a good place for the heroine of a modern novel to stay at. The heroine of the modern novel is always 'divinely tall', and she is ever 'drawing herself up to her full height'. At the 'Barley Mow' she would bump her head against the ceiling each time she did this.
>
> It would also be a bad house for a drunken man to put up at. There are too many surprises in the way of unexpected steps down into this room and up into that; and as for getting upstairs to his bedroom, or even finding his bed when he got up, either operation would be an utter impossibility to him.

Some years ago this ancient inn was devastated by fire. It is pleasant to be able to report that it has been sympathetically and skilfully restored, thatched roof and all, and that future generations of river people will be able to appreciate the Victorian atmosphere of this old pub.

Jerome has little to say about the river between Clifton Hampden and Abingdon: it was, and it still is, comparatively featureless. Abingdon is still an attractive town, but in recent years there have been developments on the outskirts that add little to its attraction. The remains of the Abbey stand on the right bank above the bridge, and as in Jerome's day the town is noted for its breweries.

There are nine churches in the town of Abingdon. St Nicholas, the one with the tower, is attached to the Abbey Gatehouse, and faces the County Hall and the market place. The most prominent feature of the town, the spire of St Helen's church, can be seen for miles. Both of these churches were mentioned by Jerome. 'In St Nicholas Church, at Abingdon', he says, 'there is a monument to John Blackwall and his wife Jane, who both, after leading a happy married life, died on the very same day, August 21, 1625', possibly of the plague, as this was a known plague year. (*Plate 19*).

Chapter 18

The memorial to John Blacknall and his wife can be seen set in an alcove to the left of the chancel. You will note that their name is Blacknall, and not Blackwall as in *Three Men in a Boat*. They are represented by two figures in black, kneeling on red and gilt cushions, with their two children kneeling behind them. The epitaph reads as follows:-

> Here rest in assurance of a joyful resurrection the bodies of John Blacknall esquire and Jane his wife, who both of them finished an happy course upon earth, and ended their days in peace on the 21 day of August in the year of our Lord 1625. He was a bountiful benefactor to this church and gave many benevolences to the poor, to the glory of God, and to the example of future ages.

. . .

> When once they liv'd on earth one bed did hold
> Their bodies, which one minute turned to mould
> Being dead one grave is trusted with that prize
> Until the trump doth sound and all must rise
> Here death's stroke even did not part this pair
> But by this stroke, they more united were
> And what left they behind you plainly see
> One only daughter and their charity
> What though the first, by death's command did leave us
> The second we are sure will ne'er deceive us.

A Short History of St Nicholas Church tells us that John Blacknall left a large sum of money, of which half the income is given to the church.

Until about 1980 loaves of bread provided for in his will were placed on this tomb each Sunday, and given away after morning service. Nowadays only on special occasions is the bread distributed by the local school.

St Helen's Church, the one with the spire, stands within a few yards of the Thames. Jerome said that in this church 'it is recorded that W. Lee, who died in 1637 "had in his lifetime issue from his loins two hundred lacking but three".' This achievement is recorded not, as might be imagined, in a stained glass window or on a brass plate, but on a wooden panel, on which is painted a genealogical tree with the names of Mr Lee's descendants inscribed in circles, which hang on the tree in the form of fruit.

The panel, in a gilt frame, measures about 3 feet by 2 feet 6 inches. At the top is inscribed 'all the Glory to God only' and in the middle, surrounded by the branches of the tree, is the portrait of William Lee.

'From Clifton to Culham' Jerome says 'the river banks are flat, monotonous and uninteresting, but, after you get through Culham lock – the coldest and deepest lock on the river – the landscape improves.' Opinion seems to have been unanimous that it was the coldest lock, for both Thacker and Armstrong described it as such: But Thacker disagrees with the statement that it was the deepest, and awards the distinction to Sandford.

The bridge and cottage at Nuneham Courtenay were a favourite excursion for Victorians. The bridge marked the site of an old lock; in the guide books it was always referred to as the 'lock'. This lock, which was really a flash weir, was in existence in the early part of the nineteenth century. Jerome said the park could be viewed on Tuesdays and Thursdays, and this is confirmed by Dickens' *Dictionary of the Thames*.

Admission was by ticket, and each ticket admitted ten persons to the lock and Carfax. By the 'lock' was meant the cottage, where parties could obtain tea and refreshments. Carfax Conduit was removed from the High Street in Oxford in 1787. Hence the name Carfax, which is still given to the junction of the streets in Oxford. The great house at Nuneham Courtenay was not shown to casual visitors, but permission could be obtained to visit the gardens, by making prior application to the owner.

Below are examples of the wording of tickets of admission, signed by Mr E.W. Harcourt:

> Available only for Thursday, August 10th 1882.
> Permit Mr. Rawlins and ten friends to land at
> Nuneham Lock. This ticket gives admission to
> the Lock and Carfax

Available only for Tuesday, August 8th 1882.
Permit Mr. Rawlins and friends to land at
Nuneham Lock. This ticket gives admission
to the Lock, Carfax and the Private Gardens.

The obelisk alongside Sandford Lasher, which Jerome tells us 'marks the spot where two men have already been drowned, while bathing there', can still be seen, though as it is some distance from the lock you can easily pass by without noticing it. The drowned men were undergraduates at Oxford, one of them being the son of Dr Gaisford, Dean of Christ Church. The tragedy occurred about forty years before Jerome and his companions passed that way.

Jerome was disappointed with Iffley Lock and Mill, which at that time were favourite subjects of artists. He comments, 'Few things, I have noticed, come quite up to the pictures of them, in this world.' There have been big changes here since the 1880s. In 1908 Iffley Mill was burnt down, and in 1924 the Thames Conservancy rebuilt Iffley Lock, making extensive alterations to the lock island and the weir stream. At the same time they carried out certain work to the banks of the river up to Oxford, improving this section that Jerome claimed was 'the most difficult bit of the river I know.'

Chapter 19 Jerome tells us they spent two very pleasant days at Oxford. No doubt the party put up at an hotel and left their skiff moored at Salters' yard, just by Folly Bridge. The yard is still there, and the view downstream from the bridge is today much as it was then except for the college barges, that have almost disappeared. It is one of the unchanging Thames scenes, and every feature of it has been familiar to generations of undergraduates.

On their return journey, during which it rained incessantly, they spent the first night just below Day's Lock. On the second day, with rain still falling, they began to discuss the arrangements for the evening when they were a little past Goring: and we get the first hint that their determination to finish the trip was weakening. This discussion would have started in the neighbourhood of the Grotto at Basildon, and it is reasonable to suppose that their gloom was added to by the tragic associations of the spot, for it was here that the body of the drowned woman had been found about a week before, and it was amidst Hartslock Woods – which no doubt looked damp and dismal as they paddled past – that she had spent the last hours of her life.

The reminder of this tragedy would have been the last straw. I feel sure that it was here that the thought of the lights and the life at the Alhambra proved irresistible. The Alhambra, or to give its full title, the Royal Alhambra Palace Theatre, faced Leicester Square on the site now occupied by the Odeon Cinema. It was at the Alhambra that Harriett Buswell, the victim of the Great Coram Street murder, passed her last evening. Jerome makes reference to this gruesome event by accusing Biggs's boy of having been responsible. Again, we shall hear more of Harriett in a later chapter of this work.

Thus by coincidence Jerome and his companions, on the last day of their river trip – visited the places associated with the final hours on this earth of the two girls involved in the tragedies recorded in that happy book –*Three Men in a Boat.*

PART TWO
JEROME AND ASSOCIATES

Jerome and Associates

IN THE TRACKS OF JEROME K. JEROME

Jerome was born at Walsall on 2nd May 1859. His father, whose inclination and talents leaned towards religion, was described as an independent preacher, but he was also at one time the owner of coal mines at Cannock Chase. In the autobiographical *My Life and Times*, which was written in 1925, Jerome hints that his father neglected business for religion. By the time he was one year old the family fortune had gone and they moved to the East End of London, where his father set up as a wholesale ironmonger. For years life was hard for the Jerome family.

People have been puzzled by Jerome's unusual middle name. The following letter appeared in *The Times* a few days after his death:

> It might interest your readers to know the origin of Mr Jerome K. Jerome's middle name. . . . When the fort of Komarom surrendered on October 3rd 1849, during the Hungarian War of Independence, the Press of the whole world glorified George Klapka, the courageous young General of Artillery, 29 years old at the time, who was able to hold the fort against the united Austrian and Russian armies and only surrendered when he secured an amnesty for his fellow combatants. After the surrender Klapka went abroad. When he arrived in London, Francis Pulszky, Kossiuth's Secretary, considering the young hero's precarious position, advised him to write his memoirs for Messrs. Chapman and Hall, the publishers, who immediately granted him an advance of £100. It was a question now of finding a quiet retreat, as the book had to be finished within two months. Klapka gladly accepted the invitation of the Rev. Jerome Jerome. In Walsall he found a home, and even in later years, whenever tired of restless wandering, he always returned to his kind host. When, in 1859, a son was born to the Rev. J. Jerome, in honour of his famous guest he named him Jerome Klapka.
>
> Professor Michael M. Balint,
> 1 Nemetvolgyi UT42, Budapest

Jerome senior's full name was Jerome Clapp Jerome; possibly the similarity of the middle names was a coincidence. Many people believe the name Klapka is Danish, but perhaps they have confused it with Clapp. In *My Life and Times*, Jerome tells us that when his father was married he brought his bride to his farm in Devonshire. 'It lies on the north side of the river above Bideford, and is marked by a ruined tower, near to which, years ago, relics were discovered proving beyond all doubt that the Founder of our House was one "Clapa", a Dane, who had obtained property in the neighbourhood about the year Anno Domini one thousand.' As may be imagined, two Jerome Jeromes in one family led to misunderstandings, and in order to distinguish one from the other Jerome, as a boy, was called Luther.

Soon after the death of his father, Jerome, at the age of fourteen, left school and became a clerk in the offices of the London and North-Western Railway Company at Euston. A year or so later his mother died. She had been the dominant influence in his life, and her death left him to a lonely existence in a succession of lodgings.

Jerome apparently progressed well in his railway work, but he was of restless disposition, and eventually resigned to become an actor. For three years he followed that precarious profession, and then had a variety of jobs before turning to journalism.

His first book *On the Stage and Off* was published in 1885, while he was lodging in a house in Whitfield Street. In this street, which runs parallel to Tottenham Court Road, there are still some old houses, dating from before Jerome's day. His lodging house, he tells us in his autobiography, was 'part of Whitfields Tabernacle'. When he lived there his bedroom, the second floor back, overlooked a burial ground.

In 1755 the Rev. George Whitfield had been granted a lease of this land, half an acre in extent, for a term of seventy-two years. He erected a chapel on part of the site and it was opened for worship in November 1756. In 1780, as he could not persuade the Bishop of London to consecrate the ground for burial purposes, the Rev. Whitfield obtained several cartloads of soil from the churchyard of St Chistopher-le-Stocks, which was then being converted into a garden for the Bank of England. He was satisfied that this made the ground sacred. Burials had taken place around Whitfield's chapel since 1756, and between that date and 1823, when they ceased for a few years, a total of 19,758 interments took place. The ground was used again between 1831 and 1853; during this period there were about 500 burials each year.

After the closing of the ground, developers, aided it seems by the trustees of the chapel, made several attempts to build on the land. But each time excavation started public indignation was aroused by the sight of disinterred coffins and partially decomposed bodies, and the authorities were forced to take action to stop the desecration. For years an uneasy peace prevailed, but in June 1887, after Jerome had left his room overlooking the burial ground, one of the most disgraceful scenes occurred when the place was used for a fair. People danced on the graves, and a man was killed in a brawl. Questions were asked in Parliament and there was talk of introducing a Bill. Finally, after many months of litigation, the ground was opened as a public garden in 1895.

During the time he lived in Whitfield Street, Jerome had as neighbours, just outside his window, a total of about 30,000 corpses. No wonder that when he was on the river, or spending a peaceful day in the country, the last thing that he wanted to do was to see the graves!

Another of his lodgings was in Tavistock Place, which leads off Tavistock Square. In this square at Tavistock House, Charles Dickens lived for a time.

When Jerome lodged there Tavistock Place had presumably come down in the world, for in the first half of the 19th century a number of famous people had lived there. At No 9 lived John Pinkerton the historian, and at No 34 John Galt, who wrote a *Life of Byron*. The literary associations of the area no doubt encouraged Jerome to persist with his endeavours to be a writer. He had already had another book published, *The Idle Thoughts of an Idle Fellow*. The essays comprising it had been first published in *Home Chimes*. Jerome tells us, 'The book sold like hot cakes, as the saying is. Tuer [the publisher] always had clever ideas. He gave it a light yellow cover that stood out well upon the bookstalls. He called each thousand copies an "edition" and, before the end of the year, was advertising the twenty-third. I was getting a royalty of two-pence-halfpenny a copy; and dreamed of a fur coat.'

Jerome must have received nearly £250 in royalties in the first year of publication; a handsome sum in those days. It indicated that he was a successful writer before *Three Men in a Boat* brought him fortune and fame.

Although he did not list all his lodgings, it is plain that Jerome moved frequently. We know that in the four years 1885-8, in addition to the Whitfield Street Lodgings he lodged at Newman Street. This is a thoroughfare that runs between Oxford Street and Goodge Street.

Although he and his friends also sallied out on river trips from other addresses, we can be reasonably sure, from certain hints, that when he was writing *Three Men*, he had Newman Street in mind as the starting place of his story. It will be remembered that a small crowd collected as Jerome, Harris and Montmorency stood on the steps of their lodgings and waited, surrounded by their luggage, for a cab. Among these idlers was 'the empty can superintendent from the Blue Posts'. Halfway along Newman Street you can still see the pub referred to, although since the mid 1980s it has been known as the 'Rose and Crown'.

At first I assumed that the number of Jerome's lodgings was 42. Biggs's boy called to a friend, 'Hi! ground floor o' 42's a-moving.' The present No 42 is a furniture showroom in a larger building that obviously covers the ground previously occupied by several of the old houses. Some of the basements still exist and it is reasonable to suppose they are the originals. There has been much rebuilding, and few of the present structures date from Jerome's day.

It was when I read Alfred Moss' biography of Jerome that I discovered that he and George lodged at No 36 Newman Street. This house has also been rebuilt since the 1880s, but its neighbour, now numbered 34/5, is more in keeping with the period. The steps and railings of this building bear a striking resemblance to those depicted in Frederic's drawing of the scene of departure.

Chapter 1

In *Three Men*, Jerome called his landlady Mrs Poppets. This seems too good to be true, and so it proves, for I found in the rates book at Marylebone Reference Library that the occupant of No 36 Newman Street was Ann McNeill. The rateable value of the house was £75, and for that year the rates, at 4/10d in the pound, amounted to £18.2s.6d.

The public house, which is within sight of these lodgings, is probably the original building. When I first visited it in the 1960s, there was a large bar, with a long mahogany counter, and mirrors and carved mahogany behind; a staircase ascended from one corner. Sadly, few of the original features now remain, although the cellar contains a Victorian fireplace and the bricked-up entrance to an old passageway which once led, rather mysteriously, under the street to the nearby Berners Hotel.

Chapter 5

Clearly the reference in *Three Men* suggests that the Blue Posts was an establishment with which Jerome was affectionately familiar, presumably in preference to another pub, the Cambridge, which was slightly closer to his lodgings at the other end of Newman Street. Looking up the street from its junction with Oxford Street, the former Blue Posts can be seen on the left; and on the right, a comfortable couple of minutes walk from the pub, is No 36. At the far end the Post Office tower, looming over everything, reminds us decisively that we are no longer in the 1880s!

Mr Moss tells us that:

> When acting as a clerk to a firm of solicitors, Jerome lived in a front room at No 36 Newman Street. In a back room of the same building lived also Mr George Wingrave, a bank clerk. For a considerable time the two young men used to pass each other without speaking. The property changed hands and the landlady then suggested that it would be more economical for them both if they lived together. This they did, occupying the same sitting room and sleeping in the same bedroom. This was the beginning of a life-long friendship.

These are important factors, for if Jerome had not met both George and Harris, *Three Men in a Boat* would not have been written or, if it had, it would have been a different book. Also, by this casual introduction, Jerome gained his staunchest friend. This is no reflection upon Harris, who married in 1889, a year after Jerome, and who would have been preoccupied with bringing up a family. George remained a bachelor, and it is clear that his friendship with Jerome soon extended to include the whole family.

Everyone who knew Jerome was impressed by his good nature, his many acts of charity, which were performed without fuss or publicity, and by his Christian qualities. George, who lived with him for a number of years, was well qualified to judge. He stated soon after Jerome's death that in the years they lodged together they went for many long walks, and trip after trip along the Thames, and that he never heard him say a base word or utter an unclean thought: and he never went to bed without saying his prayers.

When Jerome was a young man he told George that he had four ambitions in life:

(1) To edit a successful journal
(2) To write a successful play
(3) To write a successful book
(4) To become a Member of Parliament

He achieved the first three. Most of us do not list our ambitions in such precise form, but if we did, how many of us at the end of our lives would register a score of 75 per cent?

It was from Newman Street, then, that the journey described in *Three Men in a Boat* began, although at the time it was written Jerome was recently married, and living with his wife at Chelsea. It was first published serially in the monthly magazine *Home Chimes*, edited by F.W. Robinson. The first instalment appeared in the issue of August 1888, and by the end of that volume the three travellers had reached Runnymede. The last instalment was in the issue of June 1889. There were no illustrations, but the text appears to be practically the same as in the book edition, published in August 1889. The main difference is in the opening paragraph, which in the *Home Chimes* version is as follows:

> There was George and Bill Harris and me – I should say I – and Montmorency. It ought to be "were": there *were* George and Bill Harris, and me – I, and Montmorency. It is very odd, but good grammar always sounds so stiff and strange to me. I suppose it is having been brought up in our family that is the cause of this. Well, there we were, sitting in my room, smoking, and talking, and talking about how bad we were – bad from a medical point of view, I mean, of course.

Compare this clumsy paragraph with the opening of the book version. That was the most important change, but throughout the book odd words and phrases were altered, no doubt by Jerome himself when he was revising the serial before it took its new form.

Like many other works of art, *Three Men in a Boat* grew, almost accidentally, from a small, insignificant seed. Jerome intended to write a guide book to the Thames, about its scenery and history, and he confesses that he did not mean to write a funny book. The 'humorous relief' that he intended should spice the narrative seemed to take over, and the result was that unique mixture of humour, pathos and potted history that has enthralled generations.

The serial form of the story apparently attracted little attention, which may account for the surprise Jerome expressed at the success of the book version a year later. Here again it is interesting to speculate what would have happened if this lack of interest had discouraged the publishers of the book. It would have existed in its monthly instalments, but would any of us have read the story – or heard of the author?

In the sale at Sotheby's in March 1968 some of Jerome's letters to Mr J.W. Arrowsmith were auctioned: they dealt with the book publications. In one of these letters Jerome said *Three Men* was 'a book I have great hopes of'. It is clear that he was negotiating with Arrowsmith's while the story was appearing in *Home Chimes*, and before it was completed.

The notes in Sotheby's catalogue explain:

> . . . the first letter offering the work '. . . a series of entirely humorous papers . . .', the subsequent letters describing it as 'a book I have great hopes of', discussing many details of the publication, lay-out and illustrations, suggesting that his status as an author makes an edition at 3/6d more advisable than one at a shilling, explaining his choice of Arrowsmith as publisher ('for energy and push I suppose the leading firm now'), sending chapters of the book at intervals and Frederic's drawings for the illustrations ('they appear to be very good indeed – full of humour and well drawn . . .'), drawing attention to the deliberately 'careless and unconventional' arrangement he himself proposes for the illustrations, and requesting the insertion of circulars in any further copies printed, etc., together with (1) the autograph text for this circular (headed 'Introduction' and purporting to describe a friend's bewildered and irate reactions to the book); (2) Carbon copies of four letters to Jerome K. Jerome from J.W. Arrowsmith . . . 25 February – 14 March 1889 answering Jerome's first letter 'Of course I recognise your name . . .'.

It is clear that even in those days Jerome had a true appreciation of his worth as a writer, and that he was not averse to applying a little soft soap when negotiating with a publisher.

It is also plain to see that he took an interest in every aspect of publication – the price, the publicity and especially the illustrations.

Perhaps this explains why Frederic's drawings reflect so faithfully the spirit of the story. The artist worked to Jerome's directions, with the result that the drawings make their own vital contribution to the book. This is confirmed by contrasting them with modern reprints of *Three Men in a Boat*, with illustrations by other artists.

In later years, Mr Arrowsmith commented on the amount of royalties he paid Jerome each year, and said he could not imagine what became of all the copies of *Three Men in a Boat.* 'I often think', he continued, 'that the public must eat them.'

Jerome was no less surprised by the immediate success of the book version than were many other people. Writing, twenty years later, a preface to the 1929 edition, he said that in addition to sales in Great Britain, amounting to over 200,000, those throughout the United States totalled more than a million. He added that as the book was published before the Copyright Convention, the American sales brought him no material advantage. He confessed that he was unable to explain such extraordinary success, and that he had written books that appeared to him cleverer and more humorous: yet they did not achieve the same universal popularity. He continued:

> I have come to the conclusion that, be the explanation what it may, I can take credit to myself for having written this book. That is, if I did write it. For really I hardly remember doing so. I remember only feeling very young and absurdly pleased with myself for reasons that concern only myself.

On 21st June, Jerome had married Georgina Elizabeth Henrietta Stanley Marris at St Luke's Church, Chelsea. They were both twenty-nine. She had been divorced at the High Court of Justice on the 12th June, only nine days before their wedding. We are told in the marriage certificate that it was on her own petition. Witnesses to the marriage were George Wingrave, who was best man, and Gretchen Hentschel, who presumably was the sister of Carl Hentschel, or Harris as we know him in *Three Men.* At the time of the book's composition, Jerome and Georgina had just returned from their honeymoon, which was spent on the Thames.

Jerome was described, in a generous obituary in *The Times*, as a 'typical humorist of the 'eighties'. This comment is perhaps more easily appreciated in our own day than when it was written in 1927. It is now one more reason for the perennial popularity of *Three Men in a Boat*: like that other classic book of the period *The Diary of a Nobody*, it spotlights an era that we look back to with nostalgia. When we talk of 'the good old days', we visualise something like the 1880s. We know that in some ways they were anything but good, but this has no effect on the reality of our feeling. The fact of Jerome's setting the story on the Thames has magnified this special aspect, for the river, even today,

CERTIFIED COPY OF AN ENTRY OF MARRIAGE

The statutory fee for this certificate is 3s. 9d.
Where a search is necessary to find the entry,
a search fee is payable in addition.

Given at the GENERAL REGISTER OFFICE,
SOMERSET HOUSE, LONDON

Application Number. 509778

1888. Marriage solemnized at the Parish Church in the Parish of South Chelsea in the County of Middlesex

No.	When Married	Name and Surname	Age	Condition	Rank or Profession	Residence at the time of Marriage	Father's Name and Surname	Rank or Profession of Father
254	June 21st 1888	Jerome Klapka Jerome	29	Bachelor	Dramatic Author	S. Martin's in the fields Middlesex	Jerome Clapp Jerome (deceased)	Nonconformist Minister
		Georgina Elizabeth Henrietta Stanley Marris	29	Divorced by Decree Nisi, Justice June 12, 1888 made absolute own petition		88 Chelsea Gardens	George Nesza (deceased)	Soldier

Married in the Parish Church according to the Rites and Ceremonies of the Established Church, by Licence or after _____ by me, Frederic Rose Cesale

This Marriage was solemnized between us, { Jerome Klapka Jerome / Georgina Elizabeth Henrietta Stanley Marris } in the Presence of us, { G. Wingate / E.F.L. Banister Goethken Hentschel }

CERTIFIED to be a true copy of an entry in the certified copy of a register of Marriages in the Registration District of Chelsea
Given at the GENERAL REGISTER OFFICE, SOMERSET HOUSE, LONDON, under the Seal of the said Office, the 9th day of December 1966.

with thousands of launches floating on its waters, retains more of the Victorian flavour than any other of our geographical features. Why this should be is not hard to understand. Although new roads span the Thames, and, near London, the between-wars bungalows line the banks, most of the topographic aspects remain the same as one hundred years ago. The hills and woods still exist, the river follows the same course; and many of the Victorian houses still stand in their shaven lawns.

If this is so, it may be asked, why is the atmosphere of the river not redolent of any even earlier period, when the same features were there? The answer is that in the 1880s the river became popular, for the first time, with the general public. No doubt the railway had a hand in this. Jerome records that when the three of them started their weekly trips they had the river almost to themselves, but that year by year it got more crowded, and they moved their starting point from Richmond to Maidenhead.

Some of the magic of *Three Men in a Boat* is missing from the book concerning their further adventures: *Three Men on the Bummel*, which relates a series of incidents in various Continental towns, or on the journeys between them. It is difficult for us to follow them in our mind's eye on their journey, and there is no connecting link between one episode and the next. Although in *Three Men in a Boat* Jerome jumps in a most haphazard way from one episode to the next, and some of them have nothing to do with the Thames, he always returns to the river in due course, which gives the book a feeling of continuity.

Jerome tells us in his autobiography *My Life and Times* that he had lived near the river for most of his life, and that he knew it well. This is evident to anyone acquainted with the Thames. Jerome, Harris and George would make river trips of three or four days, or a week. One supposes that on these occasions they seldom progressed further upstream than Reading, though they undoubtedly made an occasional foray to Oxford. A careful study of *Three Men in a Boat* confirms that Jerome was less familiar with the river above, say, Streatley. In the book, the party does not leave that delightful village until page 286, and only ten pages later they have arrived at Oxford. Indeed it could be said that so far as the river is concerned the book might as well end at Streatley.

It is true to say that nothing else he ever wrote – and Jerome was a prolific writer – duplicated his success with *Three Men in a Boat*. Nevertheless, with his novel *Paul Kelver* he was well reviewed, and no doubt he was pleased with the following reviews in particular:

> Mr Jerome has recorded his memories with the touch of the true artist. It recalls the books which chronicle the childhood of David Copperfield and Paul Dombey. *The Times*

> A book that need not feel ashamed to find itself on the same shelf as *David Copperfield*. *Standard*

A work of considerable interest, brilliant talent reminding one of the pages of Dickens. Mr Jerome's latest is probably his greatest literary effort.   *Birmingham Post*

Jerome continued to be a successful writer and editor – for he ventured into that branch of the profession and discovered a number of new authors, including W.W. Jacobs. Mixing in literary cirles, he also become friendly with many of the great writers of his time including Barrie, Shaw, Conan-Doyle, Rider Haggard and Wells. As a playwright he again hit the jackpot with *The Passing of the Third Floor Back* in 1907. In writing this play Jerome undoubtedly drew on his own experience of London boarding-houses. The leading part was taken by Sir Johnson Forbes-Robertson. In the years before 1914 he wrote several other successful plays. When war broke out, at the age of fifty-seven when many men would have considered themselves too old to don a uniform, he saw service on the Western Front as an ambulance driver attached to the French army.

Three Men in a Boat made his name internationally and enabled him to travel, and there were few European countries that he did not visit. He lived in various parts of Germany and even went to Russia. He travelled to America, sometimes on lecture tours. He was a keen motorist and took part in the first London to Brighton Car Rally. His energy seemed to be boundless.

On 1st June 1927, while he was on a car tour with his wife and daughter, Jerome was taken ill. He died in Northampton General Hospital on 14th June from cerebral haemorrhage. He was sixty-eight. In his will, which was short and simple, he left all his property to his wife; his estate was valued at £5,478.

Jerome's wife survived him by eleven years, dying at the age of seventy-eight on 29th October 1938. In her will she bequeathed to her daughter Rowena Jerome, for life, an oil painting of Jerome by De Laszlo and also one by Solomon J. Solomon. On her daughter's death the two portraits were to be offered to the National Portrait Gallery. To her daughter for life also went the English inlaid marquetry table at which Jerome wrote *Three Men in a Boat*, and a writing desk. These two items, together with the two portraits if they were refused by the National Portrait Gallery, were to go on Rowena's death to the Corporation of Walsall, of which city Jerome was a Freeman. The remainder of Mrs Jerome's property (the total estate was valued at just over £8,000) went to Rowena.

Jerome and his wife are buried in the churchyard at Ewelme, a delightful village nestling in the hills a few miles from the Thames at Wallingford. On a clear day the village is within view of Wittenham Clumps. These two prominent landmarks can be seen from the churchyard, though the roof of the almshouses attached to the church prevents them being seen from Jerome's grave. The following inscription appears on the plain stone that marks it:

In
LOVING REMEMBRANCE
OF
JEROME KLAPKA JEROME
DIED JUNE 14TH 1927
AGED 68 YEARS

'FOR WE ARE LABOURERS TOGETHER WITH GOD'
I CORINTHIANS III.9

. . .

AND OF HIS BELOVED WIFE
ETTIE
DIED OCTOBER 29TH 1938
AGED 78 YEARS

Jerome excluded from his general condemnation of graves and churchyards the tombs and monuments in Bisham church, and one feels that, although he did not mention Ewelme as it is away from the Thames, he might have taken a similarly kindly view of the churchyard in this beautiful village. (*Plate 21*).

At the Sotheby's sale mentioned earlier, Jerome's letters were sold in two lots. The first, which was the more interesting of the two, consisted of thirteen autograph letters, and brief details of their contents have already been given. They were sold for £750. The second lot, of fifteen letters and a few odd items, written between 1893 and 1897, were sold for £100. Both lots were bought by a well known American book company, and presumably all these items are now on the other side of the Atlantic, and beyond the reach of English collectors.

Alfred Moss, in his biography of Jerome, said that with advancing years most literary men experienced a feeling of regret in regard to their early works. They often wished they could be recalled. He stated that Jerome had certainly had this experience. Sir Arthur Sullivan, it seems, was also at times contemptuous of the fame that the Gilbert and Sullivan operas brought him; and he tried unceasingly to make his name as a serious composer. One wonders why the gifted – and rare – individuals who can generate laughter and gaiety should strive to be known for solemn and serious work.

Perhaps it was only occasionally that Jerome felt this way, for in *My Life and Times* he quotes with approval the following from an article on humour by Zangwill:

There is a bewildering habit in modern English letters. It consists in sneering down the humorist – that rarest of all literary phenomena. His appearance, indeed, is hailed with an outburst of gaiety; even the critics have the joy of discovery. But no sooner is he established and doing an apparently profitable business than a reaction sets in, and he becames a by-word for literary crime. When 'Three Men in a Boat' was fresh from the press, I was buttonholed by grave theologians and scholars hysterically insisting on my hearing page after page: later on these same gentlemen joined in the hue and cry and shuddered at the name of Jerome. The interval before the advent of another humorist is filled in with lamentations on the decay of humour.

Jerome wrote *My Life and Times* scarcely twelve months before he died, and even so late in life he seemed to have retained a true appreciation of the importance of the humorist. Perhaps the explanation of his ambition to produce more serious and deeper work was that, having at a comparatively early age reached the heights of fame as a creator of mirth, he wished before he died to gain equal fame as a serious writer. To a great extent he achieved this ambition in his later books and plays; yet if you ask anyone today which book he associates with the name of Jerome K. Jerome, the answer inevitably will be *'Three Men in a Boat'*.

ROWENA JEROME AND MISS FRITH

Jerome's daughter, Rowena, died in 1966. She had lived for many years with Miss E.M. Frith who, on Rowena's death, became executrix of the Jerome K. Jerome estate.

They lived in a bungalow – named Klapka – on the outskirts of Chichester, surrounded by Jerome's possessions. In the hall was his photograph, in military uniform, taken when he was serving with the French army. In the sitting room were several well filled bookcases; almost without exception every ornament in this room had belonged to Jerome. He had sought out and bought the marquetry tables and writing desks, the antique chairs, and the pictures and ornaments displayed on the walls and mantlepiece.

A visit to Miss Frith, soon after Miss Jerome's death, elicited interesting family information. The spacious rooms in Jerome's houses at Gould's Grove near Ewelme, and Monks Corner and Ridge End at Marlow, had been filled with furniture and books. Much of this furniture and many of the books had been sold over the years: the lovely pieces that filled the sitting room at Chichester were only a few of the items that he left.

Miss Frith had lived with the Jerome family for many years. During World War II Miss Jerome and Miss Frith lived first at Selsey, and then at Chichester and Oxford; and wherever they went the bombs seemed to follow them. They must have been dangerous neighbours. Fortunately both ladies and Jerome's possessions survived unscathed. Bombs were not the only danger, for on one occasion just after the house at Chichester had been damaged in a raid Miss Frith arrived home to find a stranger entering the house, and judging from his lame excuses he was after loot.

Miss Frith had a complete collection of Jerome's works, some in fine bindings and all in new condition. It was Jerome's practice, as soon as a book was published, to inscribe a copy to his wife. These volumes, published over the years, testify to his continuing devotion to Mrs Jerome. Jerome himself was reticent about his personal affairs, and even in his autobiography he tells us little about his wife and nothing about their courtship and marriage. Miss Frith, although discreet, was a little more forthcoming. When Jerome first saw his wife-to-be he told a friend that she was the woman he would marry. At that time she was a married woman, with a young daughter. She was of Spanish nationality and her first marriage was an arranged affair.

The daughter, who was five years old when Jerome married her mother, died at the early age of 38 in 1921. Her married name was Riggs-Miller. Her photograph, in a silver frame on the mantlepiece, proved that she was a most attractive woman. Jerome treated her as his own daughter and she showed her affection by adopting his name, for on her gravestone her full name is given as Elsie Jerome Riggs-Miller. They were, altogether, Mother, Father and two daughters, an affectionate and happy family.

Although a kindly and tolerant father, Jerome imposed a strict family discipline during working hours. Rowena or Miss Frith would take tea or coffee to him in his study, and if he was working they were under orders not to speak to him. He needed peace and quiet for his work.

Jerome was a keen motorist; he had driven since the very early days of motoring, and he took part in the first London to Brighton Rally. But even in the 'twenties he would not motor at week-ends, preferring to travel during the quieter week-days. On Saturdays and Sundays he enjoyed long walks in the country.

Flower-decked and brightly painted houseboats reached their heyday during the 'eighties and 'nineties. According to Miss Frith Jerome owned one, which he called *Ethelbertha* – presumably after the fictitious wife, who figures so prominently in some of his stories.

Miss Frith confirmed that George remained Jerome's firm and staunch friend. He continued to visit the Jeromes regularly, and he was regarded as an uncle by the two girls.

When I left Miss Frith, she gave me, among other items, Jerome's inkwell and pen. At the time of her death, I presented them to the Jerome Museum in Walsall.

HARRIS AND GEORGE

Both Harris and George were good friends of Jerome. They had to be, for mere acquaintances would have been mortally offended by the references to them in the book. It is accepted that we can be ruder to our friends than to strangers, as Jerome illustrated in his story of three friends who mistook a novice at punting for Jerome himself and hurled ribald comments at him until they realized their error. They thereupon apologised, it will be remembered, and said they hoped he would not deem them capable of so insulting anyone except a personal friend.

In *My Life and Times* Jerome confesses that, although there was no   **Chapter 15** Montmorency (though there was at least one dog in his life – see *Plate x*), most of the events recorded in *Three Men in a Boat* really happened; and he states that Harris and George were founded on fact.

Harris was Carl Hentschel. He was born at Lodz, in Russian Poland, on 27th March 1864 and was brought to England by his parents when he was five years old. The family moved to Eastbourne, where for a time his father owned a paper collar factory. The elder Hentschel then turned his attention to photoetching, and Carl joined him in this work when he left school at the age of fourteen. The business flourished. His father was the inventor, but it is clear that Carl pulled his weight, for when a company was formed to market the invention, Carl became the working manager. In 1887 (the year that he, Jerome and George made the main journey of *Three Men in a Boat*) he started on his own account. In his turn he proved a talented inventor. He developed the Hentschel Colourtype process, and made the first process block, according to the obituary in *The Times*, and brought about a revolution in newspaper illustration.

Hentschel's business prospered, and when in 1902 it was incorporated as Carl Hentschel Limited, he became Chairman and Managing Director. In 1966 the firm was still in existence in Norwich Street, near High Holborn. In the telephone directory Carl Hentschel Ltd was described as Process Engravers, Electrotyping and Typesetters.

In 1889 Carl Hentschel married Bertha, daughter of Mr David Posener. They had a happy marriage, and Carl claimed that his wife's help and sympathy enabled him to cope with his early struggles.

Carl Hentschel was a man of many parts. For years he was well known in the theatrical world, and he claimed that with few exceptions he had attended every London first night since 1879. It was through their mutual love of the theatre that Harris, as it seems more natural to call him, and Jerome first met. In *My Life and Times* Jerome tells us that he met Harris outside a pit door. Had this chance meeting not taken place one wonders whether *Three Men in a Boat* would have been written. Apart from Jerome himself Harris was the most important character, or at least the most prominent, and without his extrovert presence the book must inevitably have been different.

Although he must have been busy building up and running the business, Hentschel found time for many other activities and interests. He was co-founder of the Playgoer's Club; another club he founded in 1900, the O.P. Club, flourished for many years. Hentschel was its President at the time of his death.

He even encroached on Jerome's world and founded a short-lived paper, the *Playgoer*. Another journalistic venture was even less successful, for he was editor of the *Half Tone Times*, of which there was only one issue. He also edited the *Furniture Times* and *Newspaper Illustration*.

For twenty years Hentschel was an active member of the Corporation of London, representing Farringdon Without, and in 1918 was one of the City Lieutenants. Although of Polish birth, Hentschel was accused of being a German during the 1914/1918 War, and Jerome states that this brought him low. It is pleasant to be able to record, therefore, that at a dinner in the Connaught Rooms on 28th January 1919, Mr Carl Hentschel was presented with a silver tray and an address recording appreciation of the services he had rendered as the organising secretary of the London Volunteer Rifles.

Those who feel they know Hentschel from their close acquaintance with him in *Three Men in a Boat* will not be surprised to hear that he brought an unconventional and refreshing attitude to public life. As President of the Bartholomew Club in 1904 he had the after-dinner speeches printed in little books, which were distributed to the guests and taken as read, and everyone was able to settle down and enjoy the meal. This idea alone, should have ensured him immortality!

It would be interesting to know whether Carl Hentschel, as he went through life, was handicapped by the fame – or notoriety – of being one of the main characters in *Three Men*. Hentschel probably lost touch with Jerome in later years, although he was among the mourners at his funeral. It is possible that as he made his way in the world Hentschel became a little ashamed of his character as depicted, and this may have led to a certain coolness between him and Jerome. But if this coolness did develop it took some time, for *Three Men on the Bummel*, published in 1900, described a holiday the orginal Three spent in Germany.

Carl Hentschel died on the 9th January 1930, at the age of sixty-five. He left a widow and three children. He was cremated and his ashes were scattered to the winds – as he had requested – and he had asked that there should be no mourning. An obituary was published by *The Times*, and it is clear that Hentschel achieved this distinction on his own merits. Most of the account deals with his numerous activities, and, as already mentioned, he was given credit for his significant contribution to newspaper illustration. It is only in the final sentence of its obituary that *The Times* mentions that Hentschel was the original of the character named Harris in Jerome K. Jerome's *Three Men in a Boat*.

9.   The old wall at Hampton Court

10.   The Thames from The Old Wall

11. Turk's Boathouse, Kingston

12. Hampton Church

13. Ankerwycke

14. Picnic Point

15.   A Steam Launch

16.   Quarry Woods

17.　Sonning Lock

18.　The Third Shiplake Island

19. Memorial to John Blacknall

20. Goring Church

21. Jerome K. Jerome's grave, Ewelme

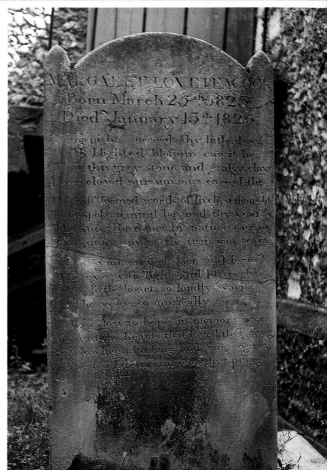

22. The grave of Peacock's daughter

This detracts nothing from Hentschel's achievements, in fact it enhances them, for only a man of unusual character and personality could endear himself to millions through the pages of a book.

The faithful George, who was present at Harris's funeral, lived to a good age, and died on 22 March 1941. He also asked that there should be no mourning, and that his ashes be scattered to the winds. Presumably he remained a bachelor, as there was no mention of a wife or family. He left considerably more money than either Jerome or Hentschel – a total of £15,069.

George, in the book, is altogether a less well defined character than Harris. He is quieter and less aggressive. And in real life he seems to have been much the same. George was George Wingrave; we know from Jerome that he worked in a bank. 'George goes to sleep at a Bank from ten to four each day, except Saturdays, when they wake him up and put him outside at two.' He eventually became a manager in Barclay's bank.

Chapter 2

Jerome indicated in *Three Men* that George had some knowledge of medical matters, and he said that this was due to a cousin, who was a medical student. In fact George's brother, Tom, was a doctor, and he ultimately reached a high position in the medical profession.

Chapter 1

There was a brief note of George's death in *The Times*, and in this case it would be true to say that he owed this obituary to the fame that *Three Men in a Boat* brought him. The report, which appeared in the issue of 25th March 1941, was as follows: 'Mr George Wingrave, formerly manager of the branch of Barclays Bank at 366 Strand, who was the original "George" of "Three Men in a Boat" by Jerome K. Jerome, died at Cheshunt Cottage Hospital on Saturday, at the age of 79.' The branch of Barclays bank still exists, though it has obviously been modernised in recent years.

George was thus the last of the famous trio to die, some fifty-two years after his literary immortalisation.

Alfred Moss, in his biography of Jerome, tells us that Harris was a gifted organizer, and that his earliest efforts in that direction were arranging trips along the Thames on Saturday afternoons and Sundays. These trips happened over several years. The author was told by Harris that nearly the whole of *Three Men* was founded upon incidents that actually took place. Here again one can speculate whether the book would have been written if Harris had not had this talent for organization, or if he had had an aversion to water.

Certain 'family' jokes inevitably found their way into *Three Men in a Boat*. Most of the readers of the book will have gained the impression that Harris was fond of drink. This would be due not only to the tale of the swans at Shiplake, when there was grave suspicion that Harris, in a solitary bout, had finished half a bottle of whisky, but also to Jerome's comments about Queen Elizabeth's fondness for public-houses and

Chapter 14

intimation that Harris was also so inclined. In fact Harris was the only teetotaller of the three. Amusing as the Shiplake incident is to the outsider, it would have been even more amusing to those in the know. When writing the book Jerome, without forgetting the wider public, had, so to speak, an eye over his shoulder, calculating the effect upon his friends and relatives.

Chapter 4   Another joke with more to it than is obvious at first sight, is Jerome's description of his attempt at packing. 'I rather pride myself on my packing,' he said; and this was, if anything, an under-statement, for Alfred Moss tells us 'He (Jerome) prided himself upon his skill in packing hampers and trunks. It was almost an infatuation with him. At one period of his life if he did not do the packing, he would not take the journey.'

In Alfred Moss's book there are several illustrations, including the following:

> Jerome
> Jerome's birthplace
> Mrs Jerome K. Jerome
> Miss Rowena Jerome
> The tablet at Jerome's birthplace

But the most interesting illustration is one captioned 'The Three Men'. Here the three of them appear in a photograph in boating attire, sitting in a meadow, perhaps beside the Thames. On the left is Harris, in the centre George, and on the right Jerome. Harris and George are leaning against a tree and Jerome reclines on an elbow. All three wear moustaches and white flannels. Harris is sporting a striped blazer, with matching striped schoolboy-type cap. Jerome wears a similar cap and a dark blazer. To a remarkable degree this photograph exudes the atmosphere of the 1880s. The group is exactly as they have been pictured in imagination by millions of readers. It is so right, and when you see it you realize what a sad disappointment it would have been if they had looked at all different.

It is possible that several of Frederics' drawings in the first book edition of *Three Men* are actual portraits of Jerome, Harris and George. On page 71, where they are depicted waiting on the steps of their lodgings in Newman Street for a cab to take them to Waterloo Station, Jerome and Harris look very much as they do in the photograph, except that they are in city, not river, clothes. The picture of Harris in the maze at Hampton Court (page 90) is even more striking, for in every way he resembles his photograph – striped blazer and cap, with white flannels. Even when he is depicted singing his comic song he is recognisable. And finally, Harris and George heading the procession back to their boat at Marlow are true to life, and Jerome, bringing up the rear, has obviously been drawn by the artist with greater care than he bestowed on the anonymous characters on either side of him.

PART THREE
THE VICTIMS

The Victims

THE DROWNED WOMAN

Jerome's story of the girl found drowned in the Thames near The Grotto, Basildon, has all the ingredients of Victorian melodrama – the girl who was seduced, rejected by her family, and who in desperation ended her life in the river. I confess that for a long time I assumed it was fiction, invented by Jerome to give balance to his book: a little tragedy as a counterpoise to the abundant 'humorous relief'. It seemed unlikely that a story that fitted so conveniently into a book of that period could be true. But even if it were, how could I unearth the long-forgotten facts?

A perusal of the local newspapers seemed to offer the only chance of finding the story. If the tragedy had occurred at the place and in the circumstances described by Jerome, the facts would have been reported in the local papers. All I had to do was to find them.

One Saturday early in 1966 I travelled to Reading, and in the Reference Library asked for the *Berkshire Chronicle* for the years 1885 to 1890. Several enormous volumes were produced, and opening the first I started on my lengthy task. In those days they believed in detailed reporting – every small incident was set out faithfully and fully. But they were sparing of headlines, and in order not to miss the vital story I had to run my eye down every column. Someone ought one day to write a book about all the human events – many of them tragic – that were reported in the local papers in the 1880s. Although I was looking for one particular story, a kaleidoscope of long-forgotten incidents passed in front of my mind's eye.

At last, after four hours, I saw a heading – it could not be called a headline, for it was little larger than the normal type – 'Extraordinary and Melancholy Case of Suicide at Goring'. A quick perusal of the report confirmed that my quest was over, and I started to copy the lengthy account into my notebook. This took 90 minutes. Now, for the first time since the incident was told in *Three Men in a Boat*, I knew the full story of the last few days in the life of Alice Sarah Douglass, and of her death, as revealed at the inquest. So far as I knew nobody else had unearthed the story and connected the true tragedy with Jerome's account; this gave me pleasure, though perhaps that is scarcely the right word, for, to tell the truth, I was much saddened by the tale. Here, then, is the story.

Alice Sarah Douglass, or to give her stage name, Alicia Douglas, was described at the inquest as a 'tall and good-looking young woman connected with the Gaiety Theatre'. The Gaiety Theatre in the Strand was noted in those days for the Gaiety Girls, created by its Manager, Mr John Hollingshead. These girls were chosen for the beauty of their faces and figures: even today the words 'Gaiety Girl' are synonymous with glamour and beauty. We can be sure, therefore, that Miss Douglass was indeed a good-looking young woman, and this may account, in part, for the sympathetic way in which Jerome tells her story.

I know little about Alice's early life. At the inquest the Coroner was concerned only with the events leading to her death. Her home was in Brighton, but she had lived in London for some years. It is plain that the temptations of city life proved too strong for her, and it was stated that she had for four years 'been under the protection of a gentleman who was killed in the last Egyptian campaign'. To add to her troubles she had had an accident to her foot and there was a possiblity she might lose a toe. These twin worries, the loss of her lover and the threat to her livelihood – for a Gaiety Girl had to be able to dance – probably account for her actions, culminating in her tragic death.

On Saturday 25th June 1887 Alice Sarah Douglass travelled by train from Padddington to Goring with a Mr Charles Jewell, whom she had met some weeks previously in a London park. She had confided her troubles to Mr Jewell, including the fact that she lived in a 'wretched hole in Soho'. Mr Jewell suggested that they should go to Goring for a time, and Alice jumped at the proposal.

It may be that the contrast between the peace, the quiet and the beauty of Goring and the noise, bustle and squalor of Soho, and the thought of ultimately having to return to the latter, combined with her other troubles, proved too much for Alice. We can guess that she had probably never before seen the upper Thames in its summer glory. Goring, nestling under the heights of Streatley and flanked by the placid, tree-lined river, must have been a glimpse of heaven. After this, how could she settle again in the 'wretched hole in Soho'? It is possible, indeed, that by taking her to Goring Mr Charles Jewell was inadvertently responsible for the girl's death. If he had chosen a less lovely spot, the thought of returning to her dismal existence in London might have been more bearable.

At Goring the couple took apartments for a month at Hill Cottage, owned by a Mr Towerton, and appeared to live happily together as man and wife. After a few days Mr Jewell had to return to London; he arrived back at Goring on 2nd July, and three days later they travelled together to London, where he took her to some lodgings in Osnaburgh Street. On the following Friday, 8th July, he called for her at her lodgings and was told by the landlady that Miss Douglass had gone to the country for a few days. Mr Jewell did not see her alive again.

Back at Goring, Miss Douglass had called on Thursday 7th July at Gatehampton Farm, a group of buildings about two hundred yards from Gatehampton ferry, which crossed the river just upstream of Hartslock Woods. Mrs Jane Gillam, who lived at the farm with her family, had several visits from Miss Douglass between the Thursday and the Saturday. She usually asked for food and drink, which she paid for, and she appeared to be desperate for company, for she asked and was granted permission to go for walks with the Gillam children. She also asked if she could stay there, and offered to pay six shillings a week. Mrs Gillam was unable to agree to this.

The amount of money mentioned is of interest, for Jerome in his account states that the drowned woman had six shillings a week to keep body and soul together. He also states that she had wandered about the woods and by the river's brink all day. He was wrong here, but only in the matter of time, for one of the puzzling features of this sad affair was that Miss Douglass wandered in Hartslock Woods and along the river bank for three days and nights. We know something about her thoughts and feelings during this time, for she left the following notes:

> Had I been able I should have done the deed last night, but meeting with a young Oxford man who so kindly talked to me [sic]. How can I forget his sweet manners? I am glad I met with him, for he unknowingly prolonged my stay on earth. I only wish I had met him before perhaps this would never have befallen me. I die so young.
>
> A.D.

> July 8th 1887. Have been in the woods all day with nothing to eat. Am tired and weary tonight. It will soon be over, and after all what have I to make me stay here? Nothing much.
>
> Sunday afternoon. Still here. Cannot bring myself to die in the river. I am not mad, and so therefore being quite sane I am backward in destroying my life. Wood and river full – boats and people. Must remain close, am so untidy and so ashamed to be seen.

> July 8th 9th and 10th.
>
> Sunday morning in the 'Lockheart' woods. Two nights wet through and no food since I left town last Thursday. For me so carefully brought up this is so fearfully hard to bear. The fearful pain of my heart, the dark and lonely woods, all add to my wretchedness. Yet, alas I would rather be there miserable than return to town where deep and unknown sorrow will be my fate.
>
> It is too hard to die young. I try to struggle against this unhappy death, and I think if some kind friend were only here now I would listen to advice. But, too late, I must die.

Another note said:

> Never shall I gain the love I have lost, and like the poet Tennyson,
> I will say –
>
>> ''Tis better to have loved and lost
>> Than never to have loved at all.'
>
> The woods today (Sunday) are fully of happy folk; some are
> singing. They little know that one so miserable is quite near. But
> I dare not show myself.

The last entry, perhaps written just before her death, is as follows:

> Mother, my dearest Mother, forgive your child. I have been much
> sorrow and trouble to you, Dearest, forgive me now. I am
> thinking my dearest of you. Father I also ask your forgiveness,
> and my brother's. I ask God's mercy and forgiveness, for I am a
> sinner. May He grant me a little mercy. If I cannot receive it, Oh
> Heavenly Father, let my soul rest in peace. Father, forgive me. I
> am so unworthy and am not fit to ask even this mercy.

Reading these poignant words after sitting for several hours in the
quiet library brought a mist to my eyes. I had to stop taking notes, for
the print was blurred. I regretted my inability to do justice to this story:
but, upon consideration, these tragic sentences need no embellishment.
Indeed, I do not think that any writer could improve on the last entry.
The words were hewn out of the girl's very soul. The story is all there:
the girl from a decent family, obviously an educated girl, who left home
in disgrace and who, in the last moments of her life had thoughts only
of her parents and her God. I feel sure that he granted her mercy and
forgiveness in abundance.

On Monday evening, 11th July, two women called at the Gatehampton ferryman's cottage and told the ferryman's son, Thomas
Bossom, that they had seen a bag and a hat beside the river a short
distance upstream. He went to the spot and saw a body in the water.
The body was recovered and taken to the Miller of Mansfield, the
largest inn in Goring, which was owned by Thoam Bower. There the
body was identified as that of Alice Douglass.

The inquest was held on Wednesday, 13th July, in the Temperance
Hall, Goring, after the jury had viewed the body at the Miller of
Mansfield. During the inquest the story was told of Alice Douglass's
unhappy wanderings for three days and nights. The verdict recorded
was, 'Found drowned'. (*Plate 27*).

As I have previously stated, I have assumed that the trip described
by Jerome in *Three Men in a Boat* was an amalgam of the various
holidays that he and his friends had spent on the Thames. But it is
possible that he had in mind one particular trip as a kind of

25. Jerome K. Jerome

26. The old Goring-Streatley bridge in Jerome's time

27. The old Temperance Hall, Goring, where Alice Douglass' inquest was heard

28.   Stuart Hotel, Great Coram Street, the site of the murder

29.   The murder room   30.   (Inset) The broken door of the second floor back

31. The Jeromes' flat, top floor, Chelsea Gardens

32. *He's Got 'em On*

backbone to the story. If this were true, and supposing that they started from Kingston on Saturday, 9th July, according to the itinerary they would have arrived at Goring and Streatley on Tuesday, 12th July, the day after the finding of Alice Douglass's body.

They stayed two days at Streatley, where they had their clothes washed after their own disastrous attempts to wash them in the river, so they would have been in the area on Wednesday, the day of the inquest. It appears likely, from Jerome's obvious knowledge of the details of the tragedy, that they attended it. There are, for instance, the significant similarities between Jerome's story and the newspaper accounts of the girl's death: apart from the mention of the six shillings a week to which I have already referred, it will be noted that he stresses that she had sinned – as she herself said in her letters – and he finishes his account by asking God to help her, which is what she asked in her last message. No doubt Goring and Streatley – two small villages joined by the bridge over the Thames, were seething with news of the tragedy, and the tiny Temperance Hall would have been crowded with inquisitive spectators (*Plates 26 and 27*). Jerome, being a journalist and a writer, would never have missed such an opportunity for gathering the raw material of his profession.

Having followed the tragedy of Alice Douglass so far I was keen to find out more about her. From Somerset House I obtained a copy of the death certificate. Her name was given as Alicia Douglass, her age 30 years, her occupation actress and cause of death 'Found drowned. Most probably suicidal.' Armed with this information I went to the adjoining department and looked in the register of births. On 15th April 1857 a daughter was born to John and Esther Douglass at 18 Goldsmid Road, Brighton. The child was given the names Alice Sarah. Her father was by trade a railway iron turner. This was the girl who through her tragic death thirty years later and the chance visit of Jerome and his friends to Goring and Streatley, was to achieve anonymous immortality: her name, until now, has been known to none, the manner of her death has been known to the whole world.

I tried in vain to find out more about Alice Douglass and her family. National and Brighton newspapers had ignored her death. I advertised in a Brighton paper for news of the family, but with no success. It is a pity, for I would have welcomed more information about her life in London and her career at the Gaiety. But perhaps any such information would have been an anti-climax and it is better to leave things as they are.

There was, however, one vital piece of knowledge missing – Alice Douglass's burial place. One fine spring day in 1966 I visited Goring and wandered round the churchyard looking at the graves. I was not surprised to find little of interest, for even if she had been buried there her grave would probably have been unmarked. From the church I

CERTIFIED COPY OF AN ENTRY OF BIRTH

The statutory fee for this certificate is 3s. 9d.
Where a search is necessary to find the entry,
a search fee is payable in addition.

GIVEN AT THE GENERAL REGISTER OFFICE,
SOMERSET HOUSE, LONDON

Application Number......14.14.90

REGISTRATION DISTRICT   Brighton

1857.   BIRTH in the Sub-district of _the Palace_   in the _County of Sussex_

No.	1 When and where born	2 Name, if any	3 Sex	4 Name, and surname of father	5 Name, surname, and maiden surname of mother	6 Occupation of father	7 Signature, description, and residence of informant	8 When registered	9 Signature of registrar	10* Name entered after registration
70	Fifteenth April 1857 18 Edward Row 2	Alice Sarah	Girl	John Douglass	Esther Douglass formerly Medley Mudley	Railway iron turner	Esther Douglass Mother 18 Edward Road Brighton	Eighteenth May 1857	Witness George Smith Registrar	

*See note overleaf

CERTIFIED to be a true copy of an entry in the certified copy of a Register of Births in the District above mentioned.
Given at the GENERAL REGISTER OFFICE, SOMERSET HOUSE, LONDON, under the Seal of the said Office, the 14 day of April 19 66.

This certificate is issued in pursuance of the Births and Deaths Registration Act, 1953.
Section 34 provides that any certified copy of an entry purporting to be sealed or stamped with the seal of the General Register Office shall be received as evidence of the birth or death to which it relates without any further or other proof of the entry, and no certified copy purporting to be given in the said Office shall be of any force or effect unless it is sealed or stamped as aforesaid.
CAUTION.—Any person who (1) falsifies any of the particulars on this certificate, or (2) uses a falsified certificate as true, knowing it to be false, is liable to prosecution.

BX 263862

Form A502X   Wt.50285/70   50M   7/65   Hw.-RE-30

CERTIFIED COPY OF AN ENTRY OF DEATH

Given at the GENERAL REGISTER OFFICE,
SOMERSET HOUSE, LONDON.

Application Number. 445526.

REGISTRATION DISTRICT Bradfield

1881. DEATH in the Sub-district of Bucklebury in the Counties of Berks and Oxon

No.	(1) When and where died	(2) Name and surname	(3) Sex	(4) Age	(5) Occupation	(6) Cause of death	(7) Signature, description, and residence of informant	(8) When registered	(9) Signature of registrar
229	Probably Tenth July 1887 River Thames Gatehampton Goring Oxon R.S.D.	Alicia Douglas	Female	30 years	Actress	Found Drowned Most probably Suicidal	Certificate received from Henry Dixon Coroner for south Oxon. Inquest held Thirteenth July 1887	Twenty third July 1887	H. Guyatt Registrar

CERTIFIED to be a true copy of an entry in the certified copy of a Register of Deaths in the District above mentioned.
Given at the GENERAL REGISTER OFFICE, SOMERSET HOUSE, LONDON, under the Seal of the said Office, the 12ᵗʰ day of April 1966.

DA 495978

walked to the river side, which is only a few yards from the churchyard, and along the towpath downstream as far as Gatehampton ferry site.

The towpath is narrow until it runs into some open meadows opposite the large white mansion, The Grotto, which in Jerome's time was a private dwelling. Gatehampton railway bridge, of red brick, spans the river a furlong or two below The Grotto, and the stream then curves gently to the right to skirt on its left bank the tree-covered hill known as Hartslock Woods. It was in this setting that Alice Douglass passed the last three days of her life. It is easy to believe that in the years since her body was taken from the river here nothing has changed. I had no hope of pinpointing the actual spot. The only information we have is that it was upstream of Gatehampton ferry cottage – this came out at the inquest – and Jerome's statement that they saw the body almost immediately after their friend's launch cast them loose just below The Grotto (*Plate 7*).

We may agree that his story of their finding the girl's body was fiction, but if, as seems likely, he attended the inquest, he would surely have an accurate idea of where it had been found. It would appear, therefore, that Alice died in the Thames between the railway bridge and The Grotto, a distance of about three hundred yards.

The ferry at Gatehampton has been closed for years, but the ferry cottage remains, a picturesque little building nestling under the slope of Hartslock woods.

I arrived early at Goring as I wished also to look around the village to find the places connected with the tragedy and found that the Temperance Hall, in which the inquest was held, still stands, and it is now Goring Branch Library. Just opposite is a cottage which I was told was Hill Cottage, where Alice Douglass and Mr Jewell stayed during their visit to Goring.

Through the parish magazine for July 1887 the burial of Alice Sarah Douglass was recorded, and there was a report of the funeral, which I quote:

> The funeral of Alicia Douglas took place on July 15th at Goring Church, in the presence of a large number of sympathizing spectators. The vicar conducted the ceremony, and Mr T. Higgs was undertaker. The father and brother of the deceased, who occupy a most responsible position in Brighton, had been communicated with, and were present at the funeral, which was of a very simple and unostentatious description, as befitted the occasion. We feel sure that the heart-broken parents have the deep sympathy of all readers in their sad affliction.

I found the entry in the burial register, though, unfortunately, there was no indication of the position of the grave. A careful study of the register yielded some useful clues. A Mr Allen Hiscock died on 22nd

July, and Herr Martin Wormser of Hesse, another drowning victim, died on 23rd July. Miss Douglass was buried on 15th July, and if burials took place in logical order her grave should be alongside Mr Hiscock's. The graves of the two men are next to each other, as one would expect, and we can say with reasonable certainty, therefore, that the burial order is as follows:

ALICIA DOUGLAS
ALLEN HISCOCK
MARTIN WORMSER

Tombstones, engraved with their names and details, mark the men's graves, but not even a mound of earth marks that of the girl.

A large tree overhangs these three graves, and its roots must be entwined around their remains. Here, a few yards from the river in which she met her death, Alice Sarah Douglass lies buried. Whenever the river floods and water rises in the sub-soil she is again immersed in Thames water.

THE GREAT CORAM STREET MURDER

Jerome made only a brief reference to the Great Coram Street murder, when he surmised that Biggs's boy, of that period, might have been involved in it. My careful study of *Three Men in a Boat* had given me great respect for its accuracy, and I felt sure that there had been a murder in Great Coram Street and that he had chosen it most carefully. It must have been a foul and bloody crime if it were to illustrate adequately the characters of 'the most abandoned and unprincipled errand-boys that civilization has as yet produced.'

Assuming that the murder might have been committed in the early 1880s, I searched through *The Times* index for those years, without success. Nor could I find Great Coram Street in an up-to-date street map of London. My next step, a telephone call to Scotland Yard Record Office, yielded useful information. A murder had been committed in Great Coram Street in 1872, the victim being a Clara Burton. Armed with this information I visited Westminster reference library, and soon found the whole tragic story in the issues of *The Times*. The murder, which was reported in detail in numerous columns of the newspaper, had apparently stirred public feeling; the sympathy felt for the victim was extended also to the man who was accused, and subsequently acquitted, of her murder.

Great Coram Street in the 1870s was lined either side with terraced houses, similar in every way to thousands of others in London. Each had a basement and ground floor, with three floors, including the attic, above. Jerome knew the type well. He tells us that his first book – *On the Stage and Off* – was born in Whitfield Street, in a second-floor back. In Newman Street he was promoted to the ground floor. In these lodging houses, rooms were rented on the basis of the higher the cheaper, with the rooms in the front being considered slightly superior to those at the back. Thus, in *The Passing of the Third Floor Back* the Stranger occupied the meanest room in the house.

So numerous were these houses that they seem to have acquired a vocabulary of their own. Their population of lodgers were continually on the move, and as it would have been difficult to keep up to date with their names it was usual to refer to individuals by the rooms they occupied. By this means the current occupant of the First Floor Front or of the Second Floor Back could be identified with ease and certainty.

One day towards the end of November 1872 a young woman moved into the second floor back at No 12 Great Coram Street, Russell Square, London. The window of this room looked out on to the small walled gardens and the backs of other houses. The newcomer gave her name as Mrs Clara Burton, but her real name was later found to be Harriett Buswell. She obviously wished to hide her identity, and as there was, and still is, a Burton Street nearby it is possible she adopted her pseudonym when she saw the name of that street.

Harriett Buswell was said to have been a good-looking and well spoken girl. Although unmarried, she had an eight-year-old daughter, who was looked after by another woman. Harriett seems to have been reticent and uncommunicative, and although she became friendly with another lodger, a Mrs Nelson, she vouchsafed no information about herself. Consequently little is known about her life prior to her arrival at Great Coram Street. During the four weeks she was there she had no settled job, but it was understood that she had at one time been a dancer at the Alhambra, Leicester Square.

The father of her young daughter made occasional payments towards her maintenance, but with no regular income Harriett soon fell behind with her rent, which amounted to 12 shillings a week. By Christmas 1872 she owed the landlady £3. Her young daughter was coming to stay with her for the holiday, and Harriett, like any other mother, wanted to buy her a present. On Christmas Eve she went to a nearby pawnbroker, T.F. Cloud of Wilmot Street, and pawned five pairs of ladies drawers for the sum of 5 shillings. A few hours later she had no money, so it seems likely that the child had her Christmas present.

Harriett Buswell's money difficulties have an important bearing on what happened later. She had been worried and nagged by lack of money since she arrived at Great Coram Street; some time before Christmas she had confided to Mrs Nelson that she was sick of life and that she proposed ending it by cutting her throat or by poison. It is evident that Mrs Nelson took little notice of these threats; in moments of depression we are all prone to make such exaggerated statements. As far as we know Harriett Buswell had no intention of ending her life. But by Christmas Eve matters had become desperate for her. It is unlikely that her landlady, Mrs Wright, would let her forget about the money she owed, and it is indeed probable that she had issued an ultimatum – 'Pay up or get out!'

Just before 10 o'clock on Christmas Eve, Harriett Buswell borrowed a shilling from Mrs Nelson and set out on foot for the Alhambra. According to *The Times* she was dressed in a manner to attract attention, wearing a black silk dress, black velvet jacket, and a dark green brigand hat, with a red feather.

At the Alhambra Harriett apparently met a man, described as a German, and had a meal with him at the theatre restaurant, the Hotel Cavour. She was well known at the Alhambra. Oscar Phillips, the head waiter, had known her for five or six years, and she was also known to two barmaids, Tryphena and Alice Douglas.

Harriett was next seen at Regent-circus (now called Oxford Circus) at twenty-five minutes after midnight (that is, early on Christmas Day) accompanied by a man, waiting for an omnibus. They caught the last

Islington & Brompton omnibus, in which there were seven passengers, including the two barmaids from the Alhambra. Harriett and her companion alighted at the corner of Hunter Street, about a couple of hundred yards from Harriett's lodgings. The omnibus in those days was a horse-drawn vehicle, known as the 'knife-board'.

Before continuing to her lodgings they called at a nearby green-grocers for some apples. In those days, when they were not troubled with shop closing acts, it is obvious that on Christmas Eve shop-keepers were prepared to remain open as long as customers appeared: London must have been a lively place at night, with the shops, pubs and gin palaces open to all hours.

On leaving the greengrocer's, Harriett took the man back to 12 Great Coram Street, and while he waited in her room she went downstairs to the kitchen in the basement. There she gave Mrs Wright a half-sovereign for her rent and received a shilling change. It being Christmas day, Harriett had a drink of stout with the Wrights and their visitors, and then returned to her room on the second floor.

There was some doubt about the time Harriett and the man arrived at No 12. Mrs Wright thought it was a little after midnight, but this was clearly incorrect in the light of the evidence of other witnesses. It must have been one o'clock or a little later.

The residents of No 12 Great Coram Street gradually settled for the night. Altogether there were twelve people sleeping there that night, including Harriett Buswell and her companion. The landlady and her husband slept in the kitchen. Mrs Nelson and Mr Nelson slept in the ground floor back parlour, Mr and Mrs Martini occupied the drawing room, Mr Fernandez had the second floor front, the room adjoining Harriett's. Mr Hall slept in the front attic, and Mrs Wright's two sons, aged seventeen and fourteen, slept in the back attic.

Early in the morning Mrs Wright and her husband heard a man clump downstairs and leave the house, slamming the front door behind him. He made no attempt to hide his departure. The remainder of the residents continued sleeping for some time. Nobody was surprised not to see Harriett Buswell during the morning, but by mid-afternoon, with neither sight nor sound of her, they knocked on her door: getting no reply and finding the door locked, they broke it open. Harriett Buswell was lying in bed with her throat cut. There were two wounds, one under the left ear and the other in the wind-pipe. Death was obviously instantaneous, and she had been dead for some hours. Although Harriett had threatened to cut her throat, it was clear from the evidence that this was no suicide, but a deliberate and cold-blooded murder.

A few trinkets, of little value, were missing, and it was supposed that the murder had been committed for gain: but the pathetic possessions of Harriett Buswell were worth only a few shillings. The stolen property was listed as follows:

> A red morocco purse, with red elastic band.
> A pair of jet ear-rings between one and two inches long, approximate value five shillings.
> A small round brooch (jet), size of a florin, female head, with cross in centre.
> A pawn ticket for five pairs of ladies drawers, pledged with T.F. Cloud, 7 Brunswick Square, on the 24th December for five shillings in the name of Jane Wright.

The murderer had calmly washed the blood off his hands before his departure. By Christmas night a watch was set on every station and port and the murderer's description was circulated: 'He is about 25 years of age, five feet nine inches high, with neither beard, whiskers, nor moustache, but not having shaved for two or three days, his beard, when grown, would be rather dark. He has a swarthy complexion, and blotches or pimples on his face. He was dressed in dark clothes, and wore a dark brown overcoat down to his knees, billycock hat, and rather heavy boots.'

Although the victim was an unknown and unimportant woman who, at the inquest, was described as a part-time prostitute, the authorities did everything they could to find the murderer. The Government offered a reward of £100 for information leading to his discovery, and this sum was later increased to £200. Various suspects were arrested and subsequently released, and it is evident that any young man with a gutteral accent and who suffered from acne was in grave danger of summary arrest. The police investigated various 'friends' of Harriett Buswell, and they even made inquiries about the person who made her periodical payments. Fortunately for him, he was thousands of miles away. In those days of slow travel this was a perfect alibi.

Public interest in the murder was intense, and *The Times* devoted many columns to the police activities and to the series of arrests and releases. The police investigation was conducted by Superintendent Thomson, Chief of the Bow Street Division, and he could not be accused of inactivity. As already mentioned, a surprising number of suspects were arrested. The inevitable crack-pot confessed to the crime, and he was remanded for inquiries: but he did not resemble the alleged murderer, and was released in due course. Every day *The Times* reported the latest developments. The police had a difficult task, and even when it became obvious as time passed that the likelihood of their catching the murderer was diminishing, the press did not become critical of them. *The Times* reported, 'evidence has been offered affecting different persons sufficient to have justified several arrests, if the Bow Street police had acted upon the principle of singling out a culprit and then fitting the circumstances to his case.' It would have been strange indeed if the police had acted in this way: but the fact that the press praised them for not doing something that was indefensible did at least indicate they were not disposed to criticise them for their lack of success.

The inquest into the death of Harriett Buswell opened on 27th December at the King's Head, High Street, Bloomsbury. The first witness was Henry Buswell, brother of Harriett. He was eighteen years old and lived at Somerset House, where he was servant to Mr Knight Watson, Secretary to the Society of Antiquaries of London. Henry had one brother and three sisters, in addition to Harriett. He told the coroner that Harriett had lived in London for ten years, and that he did not know how she got her living. When he last saw her, a few days before her death, she was in good health and spirits.

The strange events leading to the arrest of the person who was charged with the murder of Harriett Buswell deserve to be described. Ever since the murder the police had kept watch on the many foreign vessels moored in Ramsgate harbour. Presumably they suspected that one of the foreigners on board these boats, among them many Germans, might have travelled to London over the Christmas holiday and met Harriett at the Alhambra.

On Saturday 18th January 1873, the police arrested Carl Whollebe, the surgeon's assistant of the German brig *Wangerland*, which had put into port about a fortnight before Christmas. There were 163 emigrants on board, on their way to Brazil. On 22nd December Carl Whollebe, accompanied by the chaplain of the vessel and his wife, had travelled to London: they had put up at Kroll's Hotel, America Square, and stayed over the Christmas holiday. Certain actions of Whollebe on his return to Ramsgate on 4th January aroused the suspicions of the police, and he was arrested. Several witnesses had seen the murderer with Harriett and two of them, William Stalker, a waiter at the Alhambra, and George Fleck, owner of the shop where the apples were purchased, travelled to Ramsgate with Inspector Harnett from Bow Street police station.

They saw Whollebe and declared that he was not the man. At this stage the police would presumably either have released the suspect, or detained him for further questioning, had it not been for a most surprising development. It will be remembered that Whollebe was accompanied on his Christmas trip to London by the Chaplain of the *Wangerland*, a Dr Gottfried Hessel, and his wife. The witnesses, having failed to identify Whollebe, caught sight of Dr Hessel, apparently quite by chance, and were positive that he was the man they had seen with Harriett Buswell on Christmas Eve. Whollebe was thereupon released and the Chaplain was arrested.

In London an identification parade took place before the remaining seven witnesses. Only two of them, James Conolley, the greengrocer's boy, and Tryphena Douglas, one of the waitresses at the Alhambra, picked out the Doctor: the other five did not identify him. However, the police were satisfied that they had sufficient evidence and Dr Hessel was brought before the magistrate, Mr Vaughan. Dr Hessel's Counsel, Mr Douglas Straight, who defended on behalf of the consulate of the German Empire, did not oppose an application for remand, although he stated he had abundant evidence to show that on the day of the murder the accused was ill in bed at his hotel.

At the resumed trial the various witnesses were called and cross-examined. They contradicted each other as to the identification of Dr Hessel. A new witness was called by the prosecution, a Mary Nestor, a servant living at No 51, on the other side of the road immediately opposite No 12. She was cleaning the front door steps at about 7.30 on Christmas morning when she saw a man come out of No 12. She had picked out Dr Hessel from a parade of eighteen men as the man she had seen leave. She had no doubt in her own mind that he was the man. It was, she said, a light morning on Christmas Day, and the moon was shining brightly. She even noticed that his boots had plain fronts, like Wellingtons, and were very dirty.

The next day further witnesses were called, including Ernest Peter Everard Kroll, proprietor of Kroll's Hotel, America Square. He stated that Dr Hessel and his wife were staying there on the days in question. Dr Hessel was not well, and went to bed at 11pm on Christmas Eve, after which the front door was locked and bolted. The Doctor did not go out on Christmas Day, and at the time he had no pimples on his face. This evidence was corroborated by the porter at the hotel.

The Times report continues:

> Mr Vaughan, the Registrar at Bow Street, on hearing this evidence, asked Mr Poland, for the prosecution, if he had anything to urge against the credibility of the witnesses who had proved the alibi. Mr Poland had no observations on the subject. Mr Vaughan then proceeded to give his judgment, and was repeatedly interrupted by cheers from the court. He said that to his mind it had been conclusively shown that Dr Hessel was not the companion of Harriett Buswell on the night of the murder. The evidence of the witnesses for the prosecution examined at this court undoubtedly pointed at first to Dr Hessel, and justified the police in acting as they had done. The case, however, had received the most thorough investigation and the witnesses on both sides had been subject to a searching cross-examination. He was, therefore, satisfied that the witnesses who had identified Dr Hessel as having been in the company of the unfortunate woman on the night of the murder

were in error entirely. But even if their evidence had been stronger and free from discrepancies he should have considered that the evidence for the prosecution had been totally destroyed by that offered for the defence. It was, therefore, his duty and one extremely satisfactory to him, to release Dr Hessel and, as far as could be ascertained he would leave the Court free from suspicion.

The Doctor was loudly cheered in court, and all down the passages, and the crowd in the street also cheered him as he walked up the street to his cab, which was waiting for him.

Thus, after eleven days in custody, Dr Hessel was cleared of the charge of murder. To be accused of any crime when you are innocent must be a terrible experience: how much worse it must have been for a young Protestant minister, accompanied by his wife, and in a strange country, to be accused of such a foul murder.

The sympathy of the public was aroused, and an appeal was made for subscriptions to a fund on Dr Hessel's behalf. The Queen herself caused a message to be conveyed to him, expressing her sympathy and regret that he should be subjected to such treatment as he experienced in this country; and she sent £30 towards the Hessel fund. Another contributor was the Prime Minister, Mr Gladstone. The total collected amounted to nearly £1,200 – an immense sum in those days. It was presented to Dr Hessel in mid-February at the offices of the German Consulate in Finsbury Circus. The Doctor expressed his deep appreciation of the kindness which had been shown him by the people of England, and, after speaking of the shock which such an accusation had been alike to him and his young wife, he said he would send half the money to his father in Germany, and invest the remainder for the benefit of his wife. The next day Dr Hessel was the guest of honour of the German Gymnastic Society at a gathering in London.

In the press there was much criticism, not of the police, who were generally considered to have acted properly, but of defects in the law regarding the treatment of persons under arrest but not convicted of crime. The *Graphic* of February 1873 commented as follows:

> If the subscriptions which are being raised for Dr Hessel should fail to recompense that unfortunate gentleman for the pain and humiliation inflicted upon him, he will at least have the consolation of reflecting that his case will in all probability lead to a beneficial change in our mode of dealing with accused persons not yet convicted.

This paper goes on to say that Dr Hessel had been acquitted of the charge, having proved, perhaps, the clearest alibi that ever was proved in a court of justice.

In Harriett Buswell's death certificate it was recorded that the inquest was held on 27th December 1872, 3rd, 6th, 15th, 29th January and 3rd February 1873. Cause of death was given as 'Wilful murder by cutting throat'.

During the inquest a number of anonymous letters were received by the Coroner, Dr Lankester. In each case the writer was trying to be helpful, and it is not obvious why they were not willing to sign their names. The first letter suggests the possibility of one of the male lodgers at No 12 Great Coram Street having committed the murder in a fit of jealousy after Harriett Buswell's companion had left the house. The writer was doubtful whether the deed could have been done without waking the person in the next room: which casts suspicion on Mr Fernandez, who slept in the second floor front.

Another shy correspondent, who seemed not as well balanced as the first, suggested a course of action 'which I believe is almost the last stone left unturned in trying to discover the infernal fiend who committed the late horrid murder in Great Coram Street.' He recommended that all landladies should be asked to tell the police about any lodger answering the description of the wanted man who did not sleep at home on the night of the murder. He signed himself 'A Friend of the Police'.

The third letter was from a man who appeared to know something about No 12 Great Coram Street. He suggested that 'no misunderstanding should be allowed to exist as to the true character of the house where the murder of Harriett Buswell took place.' He named two women, a Mrs Waller and 'Emma' who lived there and were, he alleged, 'gay women'.

The murderer was never discovered. In spite of all the efforts of the police, in spite of the £200 reward, in spite of the fact that many people had seen the murderer with Harriett Buswell, he was never brought to trial and, so far as we know, he took his secret to the grave. If he lived the allotted three score and ten years he would have died about 1917.

Although this crime is forgotten today, it was of sufficient interest to merit mention in several books dealing with crimes and criminals. Mr H.T.F. Rhodes in his book *The Criminals we Deserve* published in 1937, referring to the murder, and to the acquittal of Dr Hessel, states 'Dr Hessel, with the proceeds of the subscription in his pocket – a handsome sum even after deducting the cost of his defence – departed, covered with honour, for Brazil. It is exceedingly probable that he was guilty after all. Great doubt has been thrown upon the alibi and the credibility of the witnesses. What they said was true but their description of his movements belonged not to the day of the murder but to another day. It is an old trick, and it is very often successful.' Mr Rhodes gives no evidence for this statement about Dr Hessel's guilt. When one considers all the circumstances of this case, including the unexpected identification of Dr Hessel on board the Brig *Wangerland*

– remembering that up to that moment he had not been a suspect – it is difficult to agree with Mr Rhodes's statement. Most people would demand very much stronger and more convincing evidence before assuming that a minister of the Church was capable of such a crime.

Three other books, published between 1920 and 1948, refer to this murder, though none of them agrees with Mr Rhodes in his indictment of Dr Hessel. But all of them refer to one detail that was not reported in the newspapers. In the murder room a partly-eaten apple was found, on which teeth marks were clearly visible. It was proved that these marks could not have been made by Harriett Buswell, and as the fruit had been purchased by her and her companion on their way to 12 Great Coram Street early on Christmas morning, there can be no doubt that the half-eaten apple was a clue to the murderer.

The three books concerned were:

(1) *Echoes of Causes Célèbres*, by Arthur Lambton.

After referring to the half-eaten apple the author continues, 'To show how thorough were the methods of the police, a plaster cast of the apple and the indentations was made, and it is to be seen to this day at Scotland Yard.'

(2) *A Casebook of Crime*, by Alan Brock.

This book mentions the half-eaten apple, but does not state that it, or a plaster cast, can be seen at Scotland Yard.

(3) *The Police Encyclopaedia* by H.L. Adam.

'The shrivelled relic of this apple, and two plaster casts of it, are still to be seen in the Black Museum.'

In the hope that I might be allowed to see these items in the Black Museum I wrote to the Commissioner of Police of the Metropolis at Scotland Yard. I half expected to be told that members of the public are never allowed into this museum, but I did not expect to receive the following reply:

... I am sorry to inform you that you are under a misapprehension about the whereabouts of this piece of evidence; the plaster cast is not among the exhibits in the Black Museum at New Scotland Yard.

Today it would be possible to identify teeth-marks as easily as finger-prints, but unfortunately in those days detection methods were not so advanced, and this evidence was valueless. I do not suggest that even if the marks on the apple could have been identified the murderer would have been discovered, but they could perhaps have proved that Dr Hessel was not the murderer, and thus have saved him from an unpleasant – if ultimately remunerative – eleven days.

Having unearthed the long-forgotten story of the Great Coram Street murder I decided to try to find the house in which it took place. When I started this quest I had no idea whether the house still stood, or whether it had been demolished by war-time bomb or peace-time developer.

Before I could find the house – if it still existed – I had to find the street. This was not as easy as it would appear, for I had already failed to find Great Coram Street in a modern street map of London. The problem was solved when I was told by a helpful librarian in Holborn Reference Library that the 'Great' was deleted from the Street's name under a street re-naming order dated 13th January 1900. I thereupon had no difficulty in locating Coram Street on the map, and I proceeded to find it on the ground.

No 12 Coram Street I discovered to be little different from the thousands of other early nineteenth-century houses that still exist in London (*Plate 28*). From the ground – or to be more accurate, from below ground – upwards, there was the basement, the ground floor, the first and second floors and the attics. A special kind of brick seems to have been kilned for these houses – a dingy dark brown brick. Perhaps the colour is due to the London atmosphere; but how then does one account for the still-red bricks of even older houses? In the 1870s No 12 Coram Street (as I shall call it from now on) was a lodging house: now it was a small hotel – the Stuart Hotel. 'Now' was early in 1967, and the neighbourhood was due to fall to the bulldozer, for this area was being developed in a big way. Already on my first visit many stark acres had been cleared of buildings, and each day the tide of demolition moved nearer to No 12 and its neighbours.

No 12, even at the end of its life, presented a bold front to the world. The name, Stuart Hotel, spelt in neon lights, the brightly-painted facade, and the gay window boxes contrasted strangely with the empty houses on either side, which with boarded windows awaited the coming of the demolition men.

On the other side of Coram Street, like a reflection in a mirror, was another line of houses. But they were all still occupied, indicating, perhaps, that their demolition was not so imminent.

I had found the murder house: now I had to get inside to see Harriett Buswell's room. Being a hotel it would seem easier for me to do this than if it were a private house; but I could not help feeling that a certain amount of tact was necessary, for the proprietor was not likely to welcome the information that a bloody murder had been committed in one of his bedrooms.

I decided upon an indirect approach, and managed after a couple of telephone calls to contact the agents for the owners of the property. They told me that the tenants of the small hotel at No 12 were a Mr and Mrs Feletti, and that their lease would expire early in 1967, when the house, together with its neighbours, was due for demolition. Armed with this information on my next visit to Coram Street I rang the bell of No 12. While I waited for an answer I tried to imagine the unknown man, with blood still fresh on his hands, stepping on the spot where I was standing, when he left the house early on that Christmas morning nearly a century before. On the other side of the road I could see No 51, where the maid, Mary Nestor, while cleaning the front door step, looked up and saw the murderer leave.

The door of No 12 was opened by a plump, amiable-looking, middle-aged woman who I supposed, correctly, was Mrs Feletti. Her accent, as well as her name, proclaimed her Italian origin. Not wishing to worry her, nor to publicise the story of the murder, I told her merely that I was writing a book, and would like to see the second floor back. She ushered me upstairs, and on the way we looked into a small room built as an extension at the back: it could be called the one-and-a-half floor back, as it was level with the half-landing between the first and second floors. I assumed that this extension had been built since the murder, but was proved wrong a day or two later when I read in *The Times* report that Mrs Nelson, one of the residents at the time of the murder, occupied a room built over the garden as a sitting room.

The second floor back, a room about sixteen by fourteen feet, was furnished with twin-beds and the usual bedroom furniture. Although Mrs Feletti had accepted the reason for my visit without question, she seemed to have a vague idea that I was there in some official capacity, possibly to inspect the drains. 'I have nothing to be ashamed of,' she said several times; and this was indeed true, for everything was clean and tidy. This property was under sentence of demolition, yet the paintwork and decorations were in good condition. From the window I looked down on the extension below and on the small garden studded with a few trees. In the summer their leaves would hide the grimy backs of the other houses: I could well believe Mrs Feletti when she said that the outlook was 'Verra nica in the summer.'

It was a strange experience to stand in this ordinary room, similar in every way to thousands of other London bedrooms, except for its history, and to imagine the scene that met the eyes of the other occupants of the house when they broke in on that Christmas afternoon (*Plate 29*). The fireplace, which was mentioned at the inquest, was still there, though the grate was obscured by a gas fire. The surround, obviously original, was of metal ornamented in relief with bunches of grapes and other fruit. I looked intently around me, with but little hope of seeing anything that could be related to the crime: and then I remembered the door, which had been locked on the outside by the murderer, and which had been broken open some hours later. I looked at this door, and saw clear evidence that at some time it had been broken open. To be strictly accurate the door itself had not been damaged – the frame and latch had given way. A new piece of wood, about six inches long, had been inserted into the frame, and this repair, presumably carried out ninety-four years before, looked as if it might have been done within the last few weeks (*Plate 30*).

I regarded this find as evidence – if evidence was needed – that the room was, without doubt, the one in which Harriett Buswell was murdered. It is impossible to describe with what satisfaction one sees a clue of this kind fall neatly into place.

Mrs Feletti agreed to my making another visit to photograph the room, and a few weeks later, complete with cameras and equipment, I again entered it. This time I spent an hour there, taking black and white and colour photographs. I could guess where the bed would have been in 1872, and I wondered, as I pressed the shutter, whether the ghost of Harriett Buswell would be visible in the negatives, in the way that faces of dead persons are seen in photographs published in spiritualist magazines. Surely, if spirits can manifest themselves, Harriett Buswell should appear in the photographs taken in the very room and on the exact spot where she met her violent death. If human thought and human emotions, especially in moments of sudden and supreme stress, can impress themselves upon our surroundings, surely the bricks and mortar, the wood and the metal that enclosed Harriett Buswell in her last moments, would be impregnated in some supernatural way with her spirit?

I must confess, however, that the shade of Harriett lost what was perhaps the last opportunity of manifesting itself, and that the images on the negatives were confined to the prosaic furniture and fittings of an ordinary bedroom.

Although Harriett Buswell was the star of the story, there was little I knew about her. She was supposed to have been at one time a member of the Corps de Ballet at the Alhambra, though she had had no settled job during the short time she lived in Great Coram Street. I was not even sure of her age, for it had been given as twenty-five and twenty-seven in the newspaper accounts. Her death certificate, which I obtained from Somerset House, gave her age as twenty-eight; her occupation, rather unkindly, as 'prostitute', and cause of death as 'Wilful murder by cutting throat'. The problem of her age was solved when I saw a copy of Harriett's birth certificate. On the night she died Harriett Buswell was exactly twenty-nine years old, for she was born on the 25th December 1843. Thus she was born on Christmas Day, and by a strange and tragic coincidence she died on Christmas Day. Her birth was registered at Kenilworth, Warwickshire.

According to her brother's statement, Harriett moved to London about ten years before her death, and we know nothing about her life during those years. Her sole claim to fame is in the manner of her death and the remarkable events that followed.

CERTIFIED COPY OF AN ENTRY OF BIRTH

GIVEN AT THE GENERAL REGISTER OFFICE,
SOMERSET HOUSE, LONDON

The statutory fee for this certificate is 3s. 9d.
Where a search is necessary to find the entry,
a search fee is payable in addition.

Application Number .... 16.7.5.97.

BIRTH in the Sub-district of Kenilworth in the County of Warwick

REGISTRATION DISTRICT Warwick

1844

Columns:—	1	2	3	4	5	6	7	8	9	10*
No.	When and where born	Name, if any	Sex	Name, and surname of father	Name, surname, and maiden surname of mother	Occupation of father	Signature, description, and residence of informant	When registered	Signature of registrar	Name entered after registration
	Twenty fifth of December 1844 at Kenilworth	Harriett	Female	George Bidwell	Maria Bidwell formerly Cross	Labourer	The mark X of Maria Bidwell mother Kenilworth	Twenty sixth of January 1844	G. Lanphay Registrar	

*See note overleaf

CERTIFIED to be a true copy of an entry in the certified copy of a Register of Births in the District above mentioned.
Given at the GENERAL REGISTER OFFICE, SOMERSET HOUSE, LONDON, under the Seal of the said Office, the 20 day of December 1966

BX 340275

Form A502X (S.13186) Dd.163760 1204 3/66 Hw-RB-30

Harriett's body was identified by one of her brothers, Henry Buswell. Henry had three other sisters and one brother. Their parents were dead. It is plain that Henry's employer held him in high regard, for he took the trouble to write the following letter to the coroner:

January 6 1873
SOC ANTIQ. LOND.
Somerset House,
W.C.

My Dear Sir,

Can you not dispense with my servant's attendance at the Inquest on his poor sister today and *future days*? An account of what goes on in a brothel does not tend to edification and brings him into contact with a class of people he has not been used to. He is a very well disposed lad and I want to keep him so.

This is the third time I have troubled you with a letter. But you will I am sure understand and excuse my anxiety. If you can spare him please send him back here.

Faithfully yours,
C. KNIGHT WATSON

This letter and those mentioned in the section describing the murder and the subsequent events, I copied from the Coroner's notes, which I had the good fortune to find in the record office of the Greater London Council. The Coroner, Dr Lankester, had the unenviable task of making notes in long-hand throughout the lengthy inquest, and it is plain that at times he was hard put to keep pace with the statements of the many witnesses. In consequence his notes, which cover numerous pages of foolscap, are almost indecipherable. But I was pleased to find them, for the records of many inquests, especially those of so long ago, have been destroyed.

The story of the life, and particularly the death of Harriett Buswell did not seem complete without knowing where she was buried. Unlike modern newspapers, those of the 1870s were not interested in the funeral of a murder victim. The local newspapers, which I read in the British Museum newspaper reading room at Colindale, did not even mention the murder, although it is clear that it was the biggest item of local news for years.

The last we know of Harriett Buswell was that her body was removed to St Giles's workhouse, where it was identified just before the inquest. Her parents being dead, and her brothers and sisters scattered, it is scarcely likely that she would have been buried anywhere but in the nearest and most convenient cemetery. It would be easy, I thought, to find the entry in the Burial Register of the local graveyard. But it turned out to be not as simple as that.

The central districts of London, which became densely populated in the seventeenth century, had no room for burials in their parish churchyards, and in St Pancras, which consisted then mainly of agricultural land, the necessary additional burial grounds were opened. Over the years many thousands of interments from the surrounding parishes took place in these cemeteries, until in their turn they became full to overflowing; and they were closed by an Act of 1852. In the later years coffins had been piled on each other, to within a few inches of the surface. These burials from outside the parish resulted in more celebrated persons being buried in St Pancras than in any other parish in England, with the exception of Westminster Abbey.

In 1832 the General Cemetery Company obtained authority to open the cemetery at Kensal Green, and seven years later Highgate Cemetery was opened. It seemed likely that Harriett Buswell would have been buried in one of these large cemeteries: but when I contacted the officials and asked them to search the burial registers, I was told that they had no record of Harriett Buswell's burial. I tried her aliases – Clara Boswell and Clara Burton – with no better success. And there I had to leave the matter. It was suggested to me that after the inquest Harriett's body might have been sent to a hospital, where it would have been used in the medical school.

Once I had found No 12 Coram Street I paid frequent visits to it. It had an attraction for me. I do not know why this should be, for I would not normally be interested in visiting the site of a murder. On several visits No 12 looked much the same, and then one day in June 1967 I turned the corner to find it derelict and boarded up just like its neighbours. For some reason this shocked and saddened me. It may have been due to a half-formed resolution I had made to spend a night in the murder room.

It was almost unbelievable that there could be such a change since my previous visit only a few weeks before. With its boarded windows and empty window boxes, one of which hung at a crazy angle, the house looked as if it had been empty for years.

I had a greater shock when I visited Coram Street early the following October. The bulldozers had done their work, and where No 12 used to be there was not one brick upon another. A hoarding surrounded the site and through one of the holes that had been provided for spectators I looked down at what had been the basement. Machinery and men were milling around. I was only just in time for it was obvious that in a day or two the deep and wide trench marking the basements would be filled in. There would then be no trace of the house and the only way of finding out where it once stood would be by taking a bearing on No 51 opposite.

I shared my observation point with several other rubbernecks and they seemed surprised when I took from my pocket a camera and proceeded to take photographs. Why should anyone want to record such a drab scene? I admit there was little to interest the normal photographer. My fellow idlers were not to know that the dust and rubble in front of us was part of a house in which a cruel murder had been committed nearly a century ago. A murder that hit the headlines, but which for many years had been forgotten. As I stood there I was thinking also of the ten people, in addition to Harriett Buswell and her murderer, who slept there that Christmas Eve, and who, like the house, are now reduced to dust. And, finally, I thought of Jerome K. Jerome. At one time he lodged not far away, in Tavistock Place, and I do not doubt that he had often walked that very pavement and recalled the murder when he looked at No 12. Writing *Three Men in a Boat* in his new abode in Chelsea Gardens, and searching his memory for a particularly gruesome crime that would illustrate the characters of Biggs's boys, he remembered the unsolved murder of Harriett Buswell in the second floor back of 12 Great Coram Street.

THE VICTIMS

The girls in the two tragedies, Alice Sarah Douglass, the drowning victim, and Harriett Buswell, the murder victim, had led surprisingly similar lives. They were both about the same age when they died, and they had both been members of the Corps de Ballet in famous London theatres. Alice, as we know, had been connected with the Gaiety Theatre. It is interesting to speculate whether she was there in 1880, seven years before her death, when the burlesque version of the song 'He's got 'em on' was sung in the show *The Forty Thieves* (see the last chapter of this book). It is even possible that Jerome, who had a love of the theatre, had himself seen the show, and among the glamorous chorus on the stage seen the girl whose death was to sadden him on a Thames holiday seven years later.

It may be said that this is too great a coincidence and that such things do not happen in real life. We shall never know. But there is the possibility of an even greater coincidence in relation to the two tragedies. One of the most important witnesses in the murder case was a waitress named Alice Douglass, the same name as the girl whose body was found in the Thames just below the Grotto at Basildon. Could the murder witness be the very girl who drowned herself in the Thames in 1887, fifteen years after the murder in Great Coram Street? At the time of the murder Alice Sarah Douglass was fifteen years old; not too young to be a waitress, especially in those days. It is impossible to prove or disprove this theory. There remains, however, a slight but intriguing possibility of this direct connection between the two victims.

PART FOUR
THE BOOK

The Book

WHERE *THREE MEN IN A BOAT* WAS WRITTEN

Having located several of Jerome's lodgings I wondered whether it would be possible to visit where he was living when he wrote *Three Men in a Boat*. The first clue was in the Author's Advertisement in the March 1909 edition, in which Jerome said,

> I have come to the conclusion that, be the explanation what it may, I can take credit to myself for having written this book. That is, if I did write it. For really I hardly remember doing so. I remember only feeling very young and absurdly pleased with myself for reasons that concern only myself. It was summer time, and London is so beautiful in summer. It lay beneath my window a fairy city veiled in golden mist, for I worked in a room high up above the chimney-pots; and at night the lights shone far beneath me, so that I looked down as into an Aladdin's cave of jewels. It was during those summer months I wrote this book; it seemed the only thing to do.

My Life and Times gives further information:

> *Three Men in a boat – To say Nothing of the Dog* I wrote at Chelsea Gardens, up ninety-seven stairs. But the view was worth it. We had a little circular drawing-room – I am speaking now as a married man – nearly all window, suggestive of a lighthouse, from which we looked down upon the river, and over Battersea Park to the Surrey hills beyond, with the garden of old Chelsea Hospital just opposite.

I searched in an up-to-date street map of London but could find no reference to Chelsea Gardens: and I was afraid that the area had been developed and changed beyond recognition. Wishing to find out when this happened – if it had – I telephoned Chelsea Reference Library. A helpful assistant, after an hour's research, told me that Chelsea Gardens still exists, in Chelsea Bridge road, between the Barracks and the river. I asked whether the buildings there were the same as in the 1880s. This necessitated further research; the assistant went away to consult the rates book, and telephoned later to say that the houses at Chelsea Gardens were not shown on an Ordnance Survey map for the years

1869-1878. However they were shown in a map of 1890 and judging from the shape of them they are the same buildings as at present.

Armed with this information I had no difficulty in finding Chelsea Gardens; a large brick building, obviously flats, had the name prominently displayed on it. No wonder I could not find it on a street map: I had imagined it to be a road or a close. And there, at the corner of the building, six or seven stories above the street, was the little circular room as described by Jerome (*Plate 31*). My search was taking place in 1967; nowadays the task would have been easier, as a plaque at street level commemorates the fact that he once resided there.

My next step was to visit Chelsea reference library, where I looked at the electoral roll to try to find out the number of the Jeromes' flat. Mrs Jerome's address given in their marriage certificate was 88 Chelsea Gardens. On my visit to the flats a few days before I had walked up to No 88 – I wondered whether Jerome could have moved into this flat on their marriage – but it was obvious that this was not the one with the circular room at the top of the building. I had no luck with the electoral roll. My search was finally rewarded when I looked in Kelly's Directory of Chelsea for 1889 and 1890; Jerome Jerome was listed at No 104 Chelsea Gardens. I noticed also that in No 89 was Miss Norreys, a friend of the Jeromes and a well known actress. She came to a tragic end, described in *My Life & Times*, having been taken away to Colney Hatch asylum.

From Chelsea reference library I walked to Chelsea Gardens and climbed the stairs to No 104. Jerome said that it was up ninety-seven stairs. I counted eighty-two steps to the door of No 104. In addition a few steps led to a door opening onto the roof, and the total from the street to here was ninety-eight. So Jerome's memory had served him well after a period of nearly forty years.

It seemed discourteous to knock on the front door of the flat and ask to be allowed to see the front room – particularly as I had no intention at that time of advertising the fact that a famous book had been written in it. However, I was keen to get inside, and after a bit of detective work I managed to find out the name and telephone number of the current tenant. Over the telephone he agreed to allow me to see the flat, so one fine June day I again climbed the stairs to No 104, and rang the bell at the door.

The sitting-room into which I was shown was obviously the one described by Jerome – 'little circular drawing-room, nearly all window, suggestive of a light-house'. He was describing the flat nearly forty years after he lived there, and having regard to the passage of time he can be forgiven small inaccuracies. The room is certainly small – about 12 feet by 10, but it is not circular, nor is it nearly all window. But the circular window is the main and most memorable feature of the room, and after a lapse of many years it would naturally loom unduly large in one's memory.

The view from this window has changed little; immediately opposite in the extensive grounds of Chelsea Hospital is a copse of large trees; in the summer their bright green leaves, towering even above the high flats, hide the view towards Battersea Park and the Surrey hills. No doubt in winter the view in that direction would extend for miles. Looking sharp left along Chelsea Bridge Road the bridge itself can be seen with Battersea Power Station beyond. In Jerome's eyes this would be the only important alien structure.

Looking to the right, over Chelsea Barracks, the view into the heart of London is more extensive, and it is likely he was looking in that direction when he tells us 'it was summer time, and London is so beautiful in the summer . . .'

I have had some memorable moments during my investigation of the various episodes in *Three Men* – when, for instance, I stood beside the grave of Alice Sarah Douglass, at Goring; or when I first entered the room in which Harriett Buswell met her death. But it is certain that the most memorable moment of all was when I sat in that tiny room 'high up above the chimney-pots' in Chelsea, where a book was born that was to give pleasure to countless millions throughout the world. Here Jerome, an obscure and comparatively unknown writer, sat at his desk and in a period of a few weeks achieved immortality. An event as rare as this confers a certain distinction upon the beholder – even on an interloper sitting in the room eighty years later. And in this instance I derived added satisfaction from the thought that nobody else seemed to know what I knew.

Jerome tells us he paid fourteen shillings a week for the flat – 'two reception rooms, three bedrooms and a kitchen.' The flat is still as described, though no doubt the rent has changed. Here Jerome and his bride set up home on returning from their Thames honeymoon: and in these rooms, no doubt, the Three Men sat and talked about their Thames holidays. When Jerome moved into this flat he was unknown; when he left it after a few years he was world famous. He was to bask in that fame until his death nearly forty years later. All these thoughts flooded through my mind as I sat in the room. In one corner was the current tenant's writing desk – perhaps on that very spot Jerome had his desk, the one he left to the City of Walsall. Here he decided to write *The Book of the Thames* – a title subsequently discarded – and my imagination, perhaps heightened by the associations of the room, could see him picking up his pen and marking on a virgin sheet of paper the words 'There were four of us – George, and William Samuel Harris, and myself and Montmorency . . .' These were the words that ran through my mind at the time of my visit; but I was to find out later, when I read the serial in *Home Chimes* in greater detail that the opening words in that, the first, version, were 'There was George, and Bill Harris, and me – I should say I – and Montmorency.'

In this room of many associations I looked round to see which parts would have existed in Jerome's day. The walls were covered with emulsion paint: they would have been redecorated countless times in eighty years. The polished floor of wood blocks would presumably be as it was when the Jerome family lived there, so also would be the varnished wood of the window frames. Just outside the windows was a low iron railing, of unusual design, and there can be little doubt that Jerome often leaned on this when he looked at the lights 'far beneath'. The room is made smaller by the outside wall which slopes inwards from a height of three feet, for this top flat is built into the roof itself.

I took a number of photographs while I was there, some in colour and some in black and white. Some I took of the road below, and by leaning perilously out of the window I managed to take pictures of Chelsea bridge and the river. Although in these tidal reaches it is vastly different from the quiet and peaceful stream between Kingston and Oxford, it is reasonable to suppose that Jerome gained inspiration as he looked down on the river Thames far below his sitting room.

EDITIONS AND TRANSLATIONS

Three Men in a Boat was published serially in *Home Chimes* in 1888 and 1889. Later in 1889 the first book edition appeared, to be followed almost immediately by a second issue. This complicates matters for the collector, for only the first issue counts as a first edition, a fact which is reflected in the price.

Fortunately there are small differences between the issues. You should look for the following:

(1) On the title page:
    J.W. ARROWSMITH QUAY STREET
    (Note: No number to Quay Street)

(2) On the inside page of the back cover:
    An advertisement for *Prince Prigio*
    (Note: 'Ready in October' at top of the advertisement)

(3) Three pages from the inside page of back cover:
    Arrowsmith's Bristol Library
    (Note: 37 Books listed)

If your copy agrees with the above three points you can be sure you own a first issue, first edition of the book.

The Author's Advertisement in the 1909 edition of *Three Men* tells us that it had been translated into most European languages, also into some of those of Asia. It would be interesting to see some of these books, and to find out from the various nationals why it was so universally popular. This typically English book could only have been written in England in the 1880s, and although it is easy to understand why it should please English-speaking readers the reason for its world-wide appeal is not so obvious.

By 1935 over a million and a half copies of all English editions of *Three Men* had been sold. As early as 1909 the American sales had exceeded a million. With foreign language sales, and the more recent English editions such as the Penguin, Wordsworth and Folio Society printings, it is likely that millions of copies of this modest river classic have been printed. I call it modest because I believe that that is how Jerome thought of it.

In addition to numerous foreign editions, some of which I describe below, the steady sale of English editions continues. For instance Miss Frith, the executrix of the Jerome estate, told me that during a six-month period, prior to my visit to her, 16,000 copies of a Penguin edition were sold. Most successful modern authors, with names familiar to us all, would be happy to sell their latest novel at that prodigious rate. Anyone who doubts the perennial popularity of *Three Men in a Boat*, or thinks I exaggerate when I claim it to be a classic, should be convinced by these figures.

Miss Frith told me that she received several copies of every edition that is published: and she was good enough to give me some volumes printed abroad. It surprised me to learn that new editions are still published regularly throughout the world; I was assured by Miss Frith that the book had now been translated into most languages, including Japanese.

It was when I examined the foreign editions that I became even more puzzled as to why this book should continue to appeal to generations of foreigners – people who could have no conception of the upper Thames today, still less of the river in the 1880s.

I have surmised that the perennial popularity of *Three Men* is due largely to its life-like portrayal of life in England in the 1880s, set against an authentic and true background of the river. Although one would expect this authenticity to be obvious to a resident in this country, and particularly to anyone who knows and loves the Thames, it seems unlikely that these aspects would attract someone who has never visited the British Isles. It would appear, therefore, that the book has merits that we have never dreamed of.

The following foreign editions were given to me by Miss Frith:

> TREI INTRO BARCA by the Foreign Languages
>   Publishing House, Moscow, 1955.
> TRES HOMBRES EN UNA BARCA published in
>   Barcelona in 1963.
> OBRAS DE JEROME K. JEROME published in
>   Barcelona in 1959. *Three Men in a Boat* is
>   included in this volume, which runs to 1519 pages.
> DREI MANN IN EINEM BOOT published in
>   Munich.
> TRI MUZI UE CLUNU O PSU NEMLUVE
>   published in Prague 1966.
> TRE MAN I EN BAT published in Stockholm 1962.

Some of these volumes were illustrated. I found them fascinating, especially when I discovered that I could read every one of the strange languages. Knowing the book almost by heart I had only to find a familiar word to be able to follow the story. For instance when I read in the Swedish edition *Biggs' pojke var den forsta som kom. Biggs ar var gronsakshandlare, och hans framsta karakteristikem ligger i hand enastaende formaga au skaffa sig de mest forhardade och lymmelaktiga springpojkar som civilisationen hittills frambragt*, it did not require any great perspicacity to translate it into 'Biggs's boy was the first to come round. Biggs is our greengrocer, and his chief talent lies in securing the services of the most abandoned and unprincipled errand-boys that civilization has as yet produced.' Now I know, among other things, that in Swedish *springpojkar* means 'errand-boy'. And when scanning the outlandish language in the Prague edition I know immediately that *Jak to vyjadne Harris svym obvyklym vulgarnum zpusobem, City to bude muset spolknout* was 'As Harris said, in his common vulgar way, the City would have to lump it' – or words to that effect.

It would seem that I have only to read the books to become expert in five languages.

From his correspondence with his publisher we know that Jerome took a great interest in the illustrations that appeared in *Three Men in a Boat*. He realized that they were an integral part of the book, and that it was important they should be in character. Frederics' illustrations, which capture the spirit, the dress and the customs of the period, amply justify the importance Jerome accorded them. I wonder, there-fore, what he would think of the illustrations in some of the foreign editions. The Swedish edition is the only one that tries to portray the period, and it does this with some success, mainly because the artist follows in the footsteps of Frederics'. The Swedish drawing of Jerome, Harris and George in the procession of delivery boys passing down Marlow High Street is very similar to the original. The artist has taken pains to depict people in the dress of the period, though he seems to have had little notion of the lines of a Thames skiff.

The Spanish edition has only one illustration – this is on the cover – three youths in modern dress are depicted in an ordinary dinghy, on a river considerably wider than the Thames. But this is nothing compared with artistic liberties the Prague edition takes with the Three Men. Here they appear as three pretty, effeminate lads, more akin to those of Chelsea in the 1970s. The Moscow volume has imagined Jerome, Harris and George as three outlandish characters, all with spectacles and long pointed noses. I am sure that three such strange creatures have never been seen on the Thames: I would be surprised to meet them on the Volga.

Nevertheless, this gives us a clue to the universal popularity of a book that, at first sight, would seem to be parochial in its appeal. Can it be that *Three Men in a Boat* has the rare ability to be transformed into the character of every country, so that the reader, whether he be Japanese or Russian, can imagine the truly English events in typical English countryside, taking place in his own locale – on his own doorstep, in fact?

Further proof of the universal esteem which Jerome enjoys as a humorist is provided by a recent article in *Moscow News*, from December 1994. Asked by his interviewer what makes him laugh, Vadim Zhuk, a well known theatre director, replied:

> I would like to laugh at something quite ordinary. To my mind, all nations can be divided into those that are satire-minded and those with a sense of humour. The first deride authorities, the second – the absurdities of life. Once we get our own Jerome K. Jerome, it will mean the beginning of the nation's recovery!

Envoi:
'He's Got 'Em On!'

Chapter 9   Among items of Victoriana that are sought nowadays are song-sheets with attractive coloured covers. You can pay several pounds for a copy that cost originally a modest half-crown. In the hope of finding the song 'He's Got 'Em On' – if there ever was one – I visited several shops in Soho and looked through hundreds of Victorian song-sheets. Nearly all of these songs owed their fame to the music-hall, and, as might be expected, they were often related to current and topical events.

During my search I became interested in the titles; some, like 'Dear Mother, I've come Home to die', of extreme Victorian sentimentality: and some, like 'Hunkey Dorum' with a more modern flavour. Because of its title I could not resist buying one, 'The Thames Embankment'. Published in 1870, it was written and composed by Charles Blamphin, and sung 'with the greatest success' by Little Bob, of the Original Christy Minstrels. As a sample I quote the following lines:

> The other day I fell in love,
> Where ladies all of rank went,
> With a charming girl who'd glossy curls,
> Down on the Thames Embankment.
>
> My love's bright eye when passing by,
> Like telegraphic wires,
> Thrill'd to my heart the Cupid's dart,
> While strolling to Blackfriars.

Fancy comparing your love's bright eye with telegraphic wires! The only excuse was that the telegraph, like the Victoria Embankment (which was completed in 1870) was a novelty. And this type of song strove, above all else, for novelty and topicality.

I spent many interesting hours searching through these long-forgotten songs, but I could not find the one I was after: nor did I see it listed in the song titles advertised in their hundreds on the back covers of the sheet music. At all the shops I asked about this particular song, and finally a helpful assistant at a shop that possessed a good filing system was able to tell me that there had been a song with that title, published in 1880 by Francis Bros., & Hunter. At the time of my researches, this company still existed, under the name Francis Day &

Co. At its shop in Charing Cross Road I was able to get a photostat
copy of the song 'He's Got 'em on'. It was sung with immense success
by T.W. Barrett, we are told on the song-sheet (*Plate 32*).

The chorus runs:

> He's got 'em on, he's got 'em on,
> Don't he try to do the heavy;
> He's got 'em on, he's got 'em on,
> He's the Don at ev'ry levee,
> He's got 'em on, he's got 'em on,
> Ain't he got a funny chevy,
> I declare, he's all there,
> Ain't he got 'em on.

What he had got on is not made clear.

The verses of the song were as follows:

> I hail'd a hansom cab one day,
> To drive me to Pall Mall,
> I dress'd myself up spruce and gay,
> Of course to see my gal;
> When I got to my journey's end,
> The cabman I did pay
> On turning round to my surprise,
> I heard some urchins say.

> Chorus
> He's got 'em on, he's got 'em on,
> etc.

> I thought it was my trousers that
> Were not cut in the style,
> Or else my coat look'd seedy, or
> They didn't like my tile,
> My boots are not so bad as that,
> For folk to chaff about,
> So I couldn't understand what made
> Those little rascals shout.

> Chorus
> He's got 'em on, he's got 'em on,
> etc.

> I push'd aside those youngsters, and
> I walk'd along the street,
> And journey'd on to her abode,
> Where we arrranged to meet,

I knock'd for my young lady, who
Lived on the second floor,
And the boys they kept on shouting
As she came to the door.

Chorus
He's got 'em on, He's got 'em on,
etc.

I really could not stand this, with
The young gal by my side,
I shouted for a Policeman,
And one I soon espied;
I told him of the conduct,
Of those youngsters to my dear,
He said 'Go on, don't notice them,
It's a saying they've got here.'

She's got 'em on, she's got 'em on,
Don't she try to do the heavy;
He's got 'em on, he's got 'em on,
He's the don at ev'ry Levee,
She's got 'em on, she's got 'em on,
Ain't she got 'em on.

A burlesque version was sung in a show *The Forty Thieves*, which was produced at the Gaiety Theatre by Robert Reece at Christmas 1880. Two famous Gaiety stars, Miss Nellie Farren and Mr Edward Terry sang the song:

Ganem
(Miss E. Farren)   Oh: Father when we've got the tin,
                        From out this fruitful mine,
                        What splendid togs we'll dress up in,
                        And won't we cut a shine.

Ali Baba
(Mr Edward Terry) No sixteen shilling 'bags' for me,
                        But something rècherchè [sic]:
                        'Twill make the 'nobs' go mad to see,
                        And all the ladies say!

Chorus   He's got them on, he's got them on,
                        Don't he try to do the 'heavy'
                        He's got them on, he's got them on
                        Say the girls, a charming bevy,
                        He's got them on, he's got them on,

	He's the 'Don' at every Levee I declare, he's all there, Ain't he got them on.
Ali	For colours I shall then go in Not tints too sad or wan, But rorty togs, all braid and frogs, And awful buttons on.
Ganem	I mean to give the girls a treat, As down the street I stray, And while they gaze, in blank amaze, You'll hear the darlings say.
Chorus	He's got them on, he's got them on, Don't he try to do the 'heavy' He's got them on, he's got them on, Say the girls, a charming bevy, He's got them on, he's got them on, He's the 'Don' at every Levee, I declare, he's all there, Ain't he got them on!

It is possible that Miss Alice Douglass, who had been a Gaiety girl, was in this show and sang this burlesque version of the song.

"HE'S GOT 'EM ON.

Written and Composed by
FRED. CARLOS.

Arranged by
EDMUND FORMAN.

I hail'd a hansom cab one day, To drive me to Pall Mall, I
dress'd my-self up spruce and gay, Of course to meet my gal, When
I got to my journey's end, The cab-man I did pay, On
turn-ing round to my surprise, I heard some urchins say.

F & D.1481.

CHORUS.

Short Bibliography

Adam, Hargreave L.   *The Police Encyclopaedia*
Waverley Book Co., London 1920

Boydell, John & Joshua   *An History of the River Thames,*
London 1794

Brock, Alan St H.   *A Casebook of Crime*
Rocklif, London 1948

Dickens Junior, Charles   *Dictionary of the Thames*
Charles Dickens & Evans, London,
1893 edn.

Henderson, Robert   *Armstrong of Oatlands Park, a memoir of
the late Rev. George Armstrong, with
extracts from his journals and
correspondence* 1859

Jerome J.K.   *My Life and Times*
Hodder & Stoughton, London 1926

On the Stage and Off
Leadenhall Press, London 1891

Lambton, Arthur   *Echoes of Causes Célèbres*
Hurst & Blackett, London [1931]

Leslie, G.D.   *Our River*
Bradbury & Co., London 1881

Moss, Alfred   *Jerome K. Jerome: his life and work*
Selwyn & Blount, London 1929

Rhodes, H.T.F.   *The Criminals We Deserve, a survey of
some aspects of crime in the modern world*
Methuen, London 1937

Thacker, Fred S.   *The Thames Highway, Vol II,
Locks and Weirs*
Kew 1920, reissued David & Charles 1968

Home Chimes Ed. F.W. Robinson, London. New Series,
Aug 1888 – June 1889
Lock to Lock Times, Kingston upon Thames, June 1888

Index